JIMMY CARTER
AND
THE WATER WARS

JIMMY CARTER
AND
THE WATER WARS

Presidential Influence
and the Politics of Pork

SCOTT A. FRISCH
AND
SEAN Q KELLY

With a foreword by Les Francis
and an afterword by Jim Free

CAMBRIA
PRESS

AMHERST, NEW YORK

Requests for permission should be directed to
permissions@cambriapress.com, or mailed to:
Cambria Press
20 Northpointe Parkway, Suite 188
Amherst, NY 14228

Cover Image, courtesy of the Jimmy Carter Library.

Paperback edition ISBN: 978-1-60497-778-3
The Library of Congress has catalogued the earlier, hardcover edition as follows:

Library of Congress Cataloging-in-Publication Data

Frisch, Scott A., 1964–
Jimmy Carter and the water wars : presidential influence and the politics of pork / Scott A. Frisch and Sean Q Kelly ; with a foreword by Les Francis and an afterword by Jim Free.
        p. cm.
    Includes bibliographical references and index.
    ISBN 978-1-934043-89-9 (alk. paper)
        1. Executive-legislative relations—United States—History—20th century. 2. Carter, Jimmy, 1924—Relations with legislators. 3. Water resources development—Government policy—United States. 4. Federal aid to water resources development—United States. 5. Veto—United States. 6. United States—Politics and government—1977-1981. I. Kelly, Sean Q. II. Title.

    JK585.F75 2008
    333.9100973'09047—dc22

2008020171

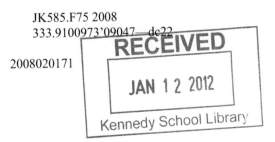

For Colin, Elizabeth, and Judy
SAF

• • •

For Sheen, the love of my life;
and for our daughter, Shriya,
who is the light of our lives
SQK

TABLE OF CONTENTS

LIST OF FIGURES

LIST OF TABLES

ACKNOWLEDGMENTS

January 20, 2007, marked the 30th anniversary of the inauguration of Jimmy Carter as president of the United States. To mark the occasion, the University of Georgia sponsored an outstanding three-day conference on the lessons of the Carter presidency. The conference reunited the former president with most of the important actors in his administration and included academic perspectives. We started with a simple conference paper but quickly realized that we had a book's worth of data. This book is a heavily revised and expanded version of our original paper for that conference. We owe many thanks to John Maltese for including us in the conference, which we both consider among the highlights of our professional careers.

One of the many benefits of our participation in the conference was the opportunity to hear the comments of former administration officials on our interpretation of the political dynamics of the "water wars." It is difficult to overstate the value of the comments provided to us by Carter's Domestic Policy Adviser Stu Eizenstat, Head of the Office of Congressional Liaison Frank Moore, House Liaison Jim Free, and Deputy Assistant for Congressional Liaison Les Francis. As we revised the manuscript, these men remained interested in providing feedback for which we are eternally grateful. And, more than grateful, we are honored that Francis and Free consented to write short essays for this book.

Successful archival research is reliant on the assistance of archival staff; we consider ourselves lucky to have worked with so many outstanding archivists. Bert Nason of the Jimmy Carter Library provided excellent help orienting us in the Carter Papers and discussing the Carter presidency at length. Kevin Ray and the staff of the Hoole Library at the University of Alabama, home of the Tom Bevill Papers, went above and beyond the call of duty helping us to get the materials that we needed. Craig Piper and Betty Self provided expert help with the John Stennis Papers at Mississippi State University. Robert Bruns facilitated access to the Tip O'Neill Papers at Boston College. Janet Bunde at New York University assisted us with materials from the John Brademas Congressional Papers. Hamp Smith at the Minnesota Historical Society was enormously helpful with the Walter Mondale Papers. The contributions of these individuals to our research are truly, deeply appreciated.

Our research has benefitted from financial support from grant funds from the Dirksen Congressional Center Congressional Research Award and the Caterpillar Foundation; our work over the last several years has benefitted greatly from the support of the Center and Center Director Frank Mackaman. Additional funding was provided by California State University Channel Islands and the Institute for Humane Studies. Research began while Kelly was still affiliated with Niagara University; funding during that period was provided by the Niagara University Research Council. Lisa Rutty provided research assistance.

Our research approach is unusually labor intensive in that it involves travel to archives—often for days at a time—and separates us from our families. Elizabeth Rothrock and Colin Frisch, as well as Sheen Rajmaira and Shriya Kelly, demonstrate an unusual forbearance for our travels, and that tolerance makes our research possible (and eases our feelings of guilt!). Furthermore, when the chips were down and funding from outside sources was not enough, the CEOs of the Frisch Foundation (Rothrock) and the Kelly Charitable Trust (Rajmaira) allowed small grants (by way of MasterCard and Visa) to keep our research moving forward.

FOREWORD

Jimmy Carter

AND THE

Price of Political Courage

In mid-April 2008, former President Jimmy Carter met in Syria with Khaled Meshaal, recognized head of Hamas, the Palestinian organization widely viewed as one of the most lethal terrorist organizations operating in the Middle East. It is also, inconveniently for many, the governing party in Gaza, having been victorious in a stunning electoral victory in that poor and volatile land in January 2006.

Israeli officials and the American administration of George W. Bush expressed shock and outrage at the Carter–Meshaal meeting, and various commentators denounced Carter in the harshest possible terms. Whatever considerations might have been behind the criticisms, surprise certainly should not have been among them.

Soon after the 2006 elections in Palestine, to which Carter was a close witness, and the fairness and openness of which he had testified, the former president told CNN's Larry King, "If you sponsor an election or promote democracy and freedom around the world, then when people make their own decision about their leaders, I think that all the governments should recognize that administration and let them form their government." He went on to tell the talk show host and his sizable audience that "there's a good chance" that Hamas, which has operated a network of successful social and charitable organizations for Palestinians, could become a nonviolent organization. There is little doubt that these observations were not designed to curry political favor at home or abroad.

Palestine is a long way from Washington, DC, to be sure (although not as distant as once thought), and conversations with the most militant advocates of the Palestinian cause in 2008 may seem a far cry from a fight over federally funded water projects in the United States three decades before, but when talking about Jimmy Carter, it is no stretch whatsoever.

Jimmy Carter has never shied away from controversy; in fact, he seems to welcome it. He is also not afraid to tackle the toughest of issues, regardless of the political consequences, and never has been. And, frankly, as one who once worked for Carter and who has tremendous admiration and affection for him still, I have come to the conclusion that sometimes he just doesn't give a damn what people think of him, his words, or his actions.

Over the course of a late January weekend in 2007, on the thirtieth anniversary of Jimmy Carter's inauguration as our 39th president, a few hundred people—including President and Mrs. Carter, Vice President and Mrs. Mondale, historians, journalists, campaign veterans, former administration officials, and "just plain folks"—gathered at the University of Georgia to recount the four years of the Carter presidency—its ups and its downs. We reflected on our times in office, we laughed at funny stories, and we got choked up at particularly poignant moments.

Most of all, we celebrated the fact that an important and long overdue reassessment of our administration seems to be under way. The second look at Jimmy Carter's term in office seems to have been fueled by at least two factors: first, of course, has been the extraordinary accomplishments of his post-presidency and the deep respect that Carter enjoys among people the world over; second, the incompetence and hubris that have characterized the administration of George W. Bush have left many Americans disappointed and in search of "good old days," wherever we can find them.

Sessions at the conference in Athens also served to remind attendees, and those who watched the proceedings on C-SPAN or who have read the transcripts since, of the many crucial and difficult issues the Carter administration confronted and the initiatives he undertook as a result: the Panama Canal Treaties, normalization of relations with the People's Republic of China, the energy crisis, hair-trigger tensions in the Middle East, the continuing struggle with the Soviet Union, the rise of Islamic extremism in Iran, the drive to bring an end to apartheid in South Africa, totalitarianism and human rights abuses in our own hemisphere, huge inflationary pressures that had been building for at least a decade, the early signs of globalization and resulting economic dislocations in key parts of our nation, updating and streamlining the civil service system, governmental reorganization, budgetary discipline, and regulatory reform, among other vital and contentious matters.

In the mid- to late 1970s, all of these issues, and others, played out against a backdrop of powerful new political realities in America, as the roles of—and relationships between—the legislative and executive branches of the federal government were being redefined in the wake of Vietnam and Watergate. At the same time, basic tenets of the Democratic Party were being recalibrated as it moved away from ideological moorings associated with Franklin D. Roosevelt's New Deal and Lyndon B. Johnson's Great Society. Jimmy Carter was elected president in 1976 precisely because his impatience with a "business as usual" approach to politics was shared by a majority of his fellow citizens. The former Georgia governor's rise to the pinnacle of national political power may have been surprising to many, but it was not accidental. Carter was the perfect candidate to run, and to win, in 1976.

Once at work in the Oval Office, however, Carter also made clear that he was equally impatient with what might be termed "public policy incrementalism;" unfortunately, from a strictly political point of view, this was not a value shared by many of the people's elected representatives in Congress, especially its more senior and powerful members. The result was a style of governing that the always wise and frequently witty former Vice President Fritz Mondale has characterized as "front-loaded pain and back-loaded pleasure."

Nowhere was this conflict seen more dramatically than in the fights over congressionally mandated public works projects, what critics long ago dubbed "pork barrel spending." As readers of this book will learn, if they didn't know before, the veto override fight over the 1978 Public Works Appropriations Bill was presaged by a 1977 battle between the Carter administration and Congress over the same issues, not to mention many of the same projects. An initial administration "hit list" of water projects became public in early 1977, and it caused an uproar on Capitol Hill. Those of us on the White House congressional liaison staff worked hard to contain the damage, while at the same time working to preserve the president's role in setting federal spending priorities and parameters.

Only a last-minute deal between the president and the then House Speaker Thomas P. "Tip" O'Neill prevented the legislative stalemate from becoming Carter's first veto. With the advantage of hindsight, those of us on the White House staff who breathed a sigh of relief when the compromise was struck—who were trying to keep relations between the two branches as smooth as possible— were probably wrong. It probably would have been better to have what turned out to be the inevitable fight right then and there.

By mid-1978, Jimmy Carter's standing with the public, and among Members of Congress, was ebbing. Of political erosion, the one that takes place on Capitol Hill can be the most damaging because it cuts directly into a president's ability to govern. Faced with that reality, several members of the White House staff hammered out a "veto strategy" as one way to reassert the president's political viability and leadership authority. Two major pieces of legislation—the Military Authorization Bill and the 1978 version of the Public Works Appropriations Bill—were identified as likely veto targets.

In fact, the president ended up vetoing both bills, and his vetoes were sustained after enormous political efforts designed and orchestrated by the White House. Extensive research by professors Frisch and Kelly, as presented in this book, examines in detail and reveals for the first time, in a comprehensive way, what went into the public works fight, which was in many ways the toughest of the two.

Early assessments of Jimmy Carter's presidency started from the premise that it had "failed," where failure was defined in electoral terms. Indeed, if the voters in a single election are considered the first and ultimate arbiters of presidential success, then there can be no disputing the notion that Carter failed; after all, we lost our reelection bid to Ronald Reagan in 1980 by a lopsided margin in the electoral college (the popular vote was not nearly as one sided, and it was further complicated by the independent candidacy of John Anderson, whose support came largely at Carter's expense).

However, a different consensus begins to emerge if the 1980 defeat is put in a larger context—if it is understood that Jimmy Carter knowingly imperiled his own presidency by the stands and actions he took. A vivid example of that character trait was President Carter's decision in the summer of 1979 to appoint Paul Volker chairman of the Federal Reserve. By then it was clear that Carter might well be facing a challenge for the Democratic presidential nomination the next year from Massachusetts' Senator Edward Kennedy; and it was obvious that Kennedy could only come at us from the left in such an intraparty fight. Carter knew that Volker would be a fierce hawk on monetary policy—that he would insist on high interest rates to squeeze inflation out of the economy. The result would be some tough times for businesses and consumers, and negative political fallout was assured. But Carter also believed that over the long term Volker and his tight-money approach would be beneficial to the country. History proved both Carter and Volker right, but it came at a huge political cost; although Carter triumphed over Kennedy at the convention, the so-called "misery index" helped defeat Jimmy Carter in the 1980 general election.

Almost without exception, Jimmy Carter was determined to do what was right or necessary despite the political downsides; those on his staff learned quickly not to try to persuade him to adopt one policy option over another based on political arguments. From inside the West Wing, time and again we saw President Carter take one truly gutsy step after another, spending his political capital in the longer-term interests of the country. If that is a definition of failure, then we should come up with better ways to measure our political leaders.

Speaking of failed presidencies, it is virtually certain that the administration of George W. Bush will be put in that category, despite the fact that he was elected to a second term in office. Central to the negative assessment will be the war in Iraq—how it was engineered and how it was prosecuted from the Pentagon (and I say that as a Democrat who supported the decision to invade Iraq and topple Saddam Hussein, and who continues to believe it was the right policy to pursue, even in view of its tragically flawed execution).

But "Bush 43" also failed when one looks at federal spending, which soared during his two terms in office, despite the fact that he had a Republican majority in Congress for much of that time. Perhaps most egregious in this regard was Bush's failure to veto a single piece of legislation because it contained too much spending. "W" and his team should have put their personal disdain for Jimmy Carter in cold storage just long enough to read up on how he took on members of his own party in Congress in order to restrain spending and to put the kibosh on bad projects. Imagine what might have happened to the "bridge to nowhere" if there had been a bit more presidential resolve and a lot less Rove-ian bluster!

When talking about the prospects for peace in the Middle East or the nature of the U.S. presidency—and much, much more—I am among those who believe that we are better off today because Jimmy Carter was once our president. I am also convinced that America will be well served by future presidents who are, we can only hope, as decent, as intellectually curious, as visionary, and as courageous as the man of quiet determination from Plains, Georgia.

Les Francis
Former Deputy Chief of Staff for President Jimmy Carter

JIMMY CARTER
AND
THE WATER WARS

INTRODUCTION

A Shot Across the Bow

In many respects, the modern Congress is like the proverbial, stubborn jackass…you have to hit it between the eyes with a 2 × 4 to get its attention. Your best (some say only) 2 × 4 is the power to veto.

—Frank Moore and Les Francis[1]

On October 5, 1978, President Jimmy Carter sent a letter to all members of Congress announcing his veto of the Fiscal Year (hereafter FY) 1979 Energy and Water Appropriations Bill. The Energy and Water Appropriations Bill had always been

---

[1] Memo to the president from Frank Moore and Les Francis, "Strategy on Various Appropriations Bills and Other Troublesome Legislation," June 5, 1978, Office of Congressional Liaison, Box 26, Congressional Veto Policy 7/29/77–10/10/79.

extremely popular with many members of Congress as a vehicle for delivering significant benefits—dams, navigation projects, flood control projects, and the like—to their districts.[2] Like the proverbial 2 × 4, the veto got the attention of Congress.

Carter's veto was the penultimate event in a nearly two-year struggle between Carter and Congress over funding for water projects. Shortly after he took office, Jimmy Carter announced his intention to launch a comprehensive review of the design and funding of water projects, and declared his intention to request—via the FY 1978 Supplemental Appropriations Bill—that Congress not fund nearly twenty water projects that had been authorized by Congress. Carter went so far as to threaten to veto the Appropriations Bill that included funding for the projects. Despite Carter's threat, Congress pressed forward. In a last-minute deal between Carter and Speaker Tip O'Neill (D-MA), Carter agreed to continue funding for half of the projects, and O'Neill agreed to drop funding for the other half of the projects from the spending bill.

Congress returned in 1978 with the FY 1979 Energy and Water Appropriations Bill that restored funding for all of the water projects. With public support for the president declining rapidly, and the perception in Washington that Carter was failing as a legislative leader, he was advised by his top aides to once again challenge Congress on funding for the water projects. This time, despite repeated warnings from key members of Congress, including Democratic Majority Leader Jim Wright (TX) and Chair of the House Appropriations Subcommittee on Energy and Water Tom Bevill (D-AL), that Congress would override his veto—thus compounding the appearance of

---

[2] On the political importance of water projects, see, for instance, Maass (1951), Ferejohn (1974), Hird (1991), and Frisch (1998).

providing weak leadership and perhaps endangering his other legislative priorities—Carter followed through on his threat and vetoed the bill. The fight to sustain the veto became a critical test of the ability of President Carter to influence members of Congress, that is, to convince the requisite number of House members to support his position by voting against the override and thus sustaining his veto. Sustaining his veto, however, would not be an easy task: the bill had passed the House by a veto-proof 319–71.

Considered in the broad historical arc of congressional-presidential relations, President Carter's veto was another attempt—in a long line of attempts stretching back to, at least, Andrew Jackson—by a president to gain additional control over federal spending and to "rationalize" water policy. While the Constitution grants the "power of the purse" to Congress, modern presidents have frequently accused Congress of being populated with wastrels, and sought, through various means, to seize increased control over government appropriations. A former adviser to President Carter emphasized that the veto was indeed an attempt to assert presidential power in the appropriations process: "I think it was a very important moment when we tried to reclaim some of the presidential power."[3] What was extraordinary about Carter's efforts was that he chose to focus on *water projects*. Many members of Congress consider these projects important for their political survival by promoting their narrow reelection interests (Ferejohn 1974), and water projects serve as powerful evidence of their political influence in Washington, further making members of Congress "indispensible" to their constituents. Presidents since Theodore Roosevelt have argued that

---

[3] Interview with Les Francis, August 2007, Washington, DC.

the executive branch is better suited than Congress to develop a comprehensive water policy that serves the economic and environmental interests of the nation. Arthur Maass' seminal work on water projects described well the rivalry between Congress and the Army Corps of Engineers, on the one hand, and presidents and the Department of Interior, on the other, for control over the design and funding of these projects (Maass 1951).

Viewed in retrospect, this particular battle between Congress and President Carter over appropriations for the water projects was years in the making. Jimmy Carter campaigned and won the presidency as an anti-Washington outsider who was especially critical of Congress, rankling many members of Congress. He was swept into office on a promise to shrink rising budget deficits and to balance the budget by the end of his four-year term. He pledged to restore fiscal discipline by reducing wasteful government spending. Balancing the budget was possible, he argued, by reducing wasteful *congressional* spending. Carter also campaigned as an advocate for the environment, believing that environmental protection and government fiscal responsibility were complementary goals. Challenging water projects fit nicely into his twin goals: fiscal discipline and environmental protection. By confronting Congress over their funding of water projects, Jimmy Carter offered the first salvo in the war against congressional earmarks[4] and pork barrel spending. One of Carter's advisers characterized it this way: "The fight against [the] water projects was the first ever effort against earmarks—pork, but the word is really earmarks—it was a shot…it was

---

[4] Schick (1995, 210) described earmarks as "appropriations dedicated by an appropriations act or the accompanying report to a particular project or activity." See Frisch (1998, 15–18) for a discussion of earmarks.

more than a shot, it was a cannon blast across the bow, on pork."[5] Another adviser offered this assessment: "On the water project fight we were thirty years ahead of our time. We were picking a fight on their turf…Carter's fight against water projects was a watershed. It began to shed light on the process."[6]

At a fundamental level, American politics was in the middle of a significant transition in the 1970s, and Jimmy Carter's presidency was an important transitional one. The New Deal consensus that had shaped American political dynamics and responses to social policy challenges for the previous fifty years was disintegrating. Americans were coming to view government as the source of their problems rather than a source of solutions to social ills. According to Stephen Skowronek (1997, 362), the challenge facing Carter was much greater than the challenges that had faced his Democratic predecessors; he needed to reassemble "the broken pieces of the party of Roosevelt and Johnson with a critical eye focused on the task of rehabilitating the beleaguered system of governance that they bequeathed to his new day." Carter was tasked with recreating an American liberalism that could compete in a more conservative political context, thereby relegitimizing the liberal vision of American government.[7] By the time Carter took office, the Democratic Congress did not fully reflect this fundamental shift in the electorate, and the congressional leadership most certainly did not; they represented the New Deal coalition that had kept the Democrats in the majority for most of the preceding thirty-seven years. Close examination of Carter's presidency lays bare the

---

[5] Interview with Jim Free, August 2007, Washington, DC.
[6] Interview with Dale Leibach, August 2007, Washington, DC.
[7] On this point, see also Kauffman and Kauffman (2006) and the essays in Fink and Graham (1998).

fragility of the Democratic coalition during this period: North versus South, New Deal Democrats versus "new" Democrats, evangelical Christians versus the mainstream religious, pragmatic politicians versus technocrats. Likewise, many of the issues raised by Carter—the congressional pork barrel chief among them—would become standards for subsequent presidents (as would energy, Middle East peace, tax reform, arms limitation, and a host of others). Reflecting on Carter's place in American political history, former Special Assistant to Carter Les Francis summed up Carter's place in history:

> He was a transitional figure; a transitional figure for the [Democratic] Party. What he did made Bill Clinton's campaign possible. Not just by region, which was important, but by ideology. He was a centrist Democrat, fiscally conservative, pro-national defense, more or less socially liberal, certainly environmentally liberal, and not wedded or beholden to many of the [Democratic] base constituencies.[8]

● ● ●

This book is about presidential influence in Congress. Presidential influence in Congress—whether presidents, through their official activities, are able to persuade members of Congress to vote with the president—is one of the enduring intellectual puzzles of the scholarly study of American politics. Inside the Washington community, presidential influence is a matter of much concern, discussion, speculation, intuition, handwringing, and folklore. For scholars and practitioners, presidential influence is difficult to divine because of the relative secrecy that

---

[8] Interview with Les Francis, August 2007, Washington, DC.

surrounds White House efforts, especially direct presidential efforts to influence the votes of members of Congress. This book is about presidential influence in the context of the rivalry between the president and Congress over the power of the purse, the power to spend money. The current battle between the branches over earmarks—which continues to escalate as President Bush's veto of the 2007 Water Resources Authorization Bill illustrates—began with this first "shot across the bow."[9] The water wars represent Jimmy Carter's provocative attempt to change the way that Congress spent money, and he challenged them on *their* turf. Carter fully engaged Congress, the White House, and himself in a high-profile battle over the way that Congress funds water projects.

By focusing on this single case—the case of the water wars—and capitalizing on some unique data, we provide substantial insight into how a modern president seeks to influence Congress. We do this by quantitatively estimating whether Jimmy Carter exercised influence on members that led to the defeat of the override motion. In contrast to casual observations of his presidency, we demonstrate that Jimmy Carter *was* capable of influencing congressional outcomes. And he was able to do so despite considerable challenges. Some of these challenges were rooted in his governing philosophy. Jimmy Carter believed that good policy was good politics. As one of his former advisers said,

> [W]hen he thought it was the right thing to do, he didn't care very much about the politics...he would look at

---

[9] Richard Nixon challenged congressional spending habits by impounding, or refusing to spend, funds that were appropriated by Congress. While provocative—his actions were found to be unconstitutional by the Supreme Court—impoundment is an administrative function that cannot modify in the long-term how Congress spends money.

> me…and say, 'I don't care about the politics, what is the
> right thing to do?' That was the way he was and that was
> his presidency."

Other challenges were created by Carter's predispositions and the
early actions of some of his staff who lacked Washington experience. Jimmy Carter was not fond of consulting with Congress
when it came to issues of "presidential prerogative," and Congress resented it; some of his staff did not regard members of
Congress with the proper level of respect, and many of his inner
circle of advisers had little or no Washington experience. Still
other challenges were beyond Jimmy Carter's control. Some
members of Congress regarded him as an "accidental president," others felt they would make a better president, and many
resented his southern and evangelical roots.

In some respects, this book is a necessary corrective to the
generally held belief that Jimmy Carter was a failure as a legislative leader. Carter chose to confront difficult issues and was
often legislatively successful; by standard measures of legislative success, he was as successful as Lyndon Johnson. This book
is not, however, a paean; it is a sober if long overdue appraisal
that focuses on a pivotal issue (the politics of appropriations and
the pork barrel), at the intersection of the two premier American political institutions (Congress and the president), nested
in a particular context and set of events. The case explored in
this book allows us to bore directly into the heart of presidential
influence in the appropriations process, while also allowing for
a reappraisal of the Carter presidency.

RESEARCH DESIGN, METHODOLOGY, AND DATA

It is about a mile, as the crow flies, between the Capitol and the
White House. Academic students of Congress and the presidency

face a similar distance methodologically. Traditionally, students of Congress tend toward quantitative studies, while presidential scholars typically gravitate toward historical approaches grounded in case studies of individual presidents. Our approach unites these often disparate methods. Adopting the case study approach, we focus on a single president. As a case study, we examine, in great detail, the political context, machinations, and circumstances surrounding the struggle between Congress and Jimmy Carter over the water projects between 1977 and 1978. Carter's veto of the FY 1979 Appropriations Bill is a fruitful case for examining presidential influence in Congress.

Vetoes are fairly rare under conditions of united party government (Cameron 2000). In choosing to veto an appropriations bill, especially one known to be well larded with benefits for members of Congress, Carter was challenging the way Congress typically did business in a very provocative manner in order to fulfill a campaign promise and assert himself as a chief executive. He was also challenging the foundation of the balance between Congress and the president by seeking to increase presidential authority in the appropriations process. In addition to these strategic institutional goals, Carter faced a short-term political reality: failure to convince Congress to sustain his veto would seal his image as a weak political leader and likely result in accelerated erosion of public support for his presidency. And former members of the Carter administration still support the contention that this was an *important*, nonsymbolic veto. One aide described the effort this way: "The effort to get the water project veto sustained was a full White House effort...it was really an all-hands-on-deck effort."[10] Another offered that the

---

[10] Interview with Jim Free, August 2007, Washington, DC.

"water projects fight defined congressional relations for the rest of the time that Carter was president."[11]

Many students of American politics (and political scientists generally) are uncomfortable with case study methodology. Chief among their concerns is the belief that it is difficult (many would say impossible) to generalize based on a single case. Close attention to case selection, however, improves our ability to generalize from a single case. We contend that the water wars represent a *critical case*—given the importance of this veto and the vast political resources expended on both sides of the fight, but especially on the part of the White House; *if we are unable to uncover evidence for presidential influence in Congress in this case, then it is unlikely that presidential influence is present in lower stakes legislative battles.*[12] During the veto battle of 1978, the White House invested significant institutional resources, and President Carter invested his personal prestige, seeking to influence members of Congress. By focusing on a "critical case," we improve the generalizability of our findings to other presidents in other political contexts.

In examining this case, we adopt a multimethod approach. Multimethod research—which is well-accepted in educational research, but has been slow to gain traction in political science—is premised on the belief that combining qualitative and quantitative data increases the ability of researchers to make inferences that maximize external validity, that is, the likelihood that observations and conclusions from an analysis can be gen-

---

[11] Interview with Dale Leibach, August 2007, Washington, DC.
[12] For an outstanding discussion of case study methodology and case selection, see Flyvbjerg (2006).

eralized to other situations.[13] In short, the use of qualitative data can both improve quantitative models and confirm model results and predictions. We contend that the multimethod approach provides a basis for bridging the gulf between the largely qualitative approach that characterizes studies of the presidency and the quantitative bent of congressional scholars.

Our qualitative data are drawn from several archival sources that provide considerable contemporary insight into political process and strategy.[14] We not only draw heavily on the records of the Carter administration, but also incorporate substantial material from congressional sources. The Office of Congressional Liaison maintained detailed records of their efforts and the efforts of the president during the water wars. President Carter's chief rival during this period was Tom Bevill, Chair of the House Subcommittee with jurisdiction over water projects. We capitalize on detailed records from his office to characterize the congressional response to Carter. We also make extensive use of detailed notes from White House meetings between Carter and the congressional leadership taken by John Brademas, the

---

[13] For an introduction to the philosophy of multimethod research, see Greene, Caracelli, and Graham (1989); see also Johnson and Onwuegbuzie (2004), and Johnson, Onwuegbuzie, and Turner (2006). The likely reason for the origin and development of multimethod research in education is that the results of these studies seek to maximize external validity to increase their relevance to classroom and administrative practitioners. Our research philosophy is somewhat similar in that we seek to address research questions in a way that is methodologically sound and casts light on academic theory while simultaneously doing minimal violence to the underlying political facts through excessive stylization. In short (if we are successful), a practitioner who reads this book will not find our approach to be excessively abstract and therefore useless in "the field."

[14] For a discussion of archival research in political science, see Frisch and Kelly (2003).

then House Democratic Whip, through much of this period. Oral histories conducted at the conclusion of the Carter presidency with the principal actors provide additional qualitative evidence, as do interviews with many of the political actors involved in this case, and other observers. To a lesser extent, biographical accounts and secondary textual sources provide additional qualitative data. Quantitative data are generated from the archival sources. Specifically, we are able to identify those members of Congress who were directly lobbied by the president (and who were also lobbied by Tom Bevill), which allows us to estimate presidential influence more directly than any past study that we are aware of. We also employ congressional roll call votes, as well as other publicly available sources of data.

ORGANIZATION OF THE BOOK

In chapter 1, we discuss the general features of the presidential veto and academic research that seeks to understand presidential influence in Congress. In chapter 2, we discuss the political context that faced the Carter administration on its arrival in Washington; we focus on the unsettled nature of the congressional context, the conflict between congressional expectations and the Carter legislative agenda, and the Carter transition and staffing of the administration. The origin of the water wars was congressional attachment to water projects, on the one hand, and Jimmy Carter's dedication to fiscal discipline and changing how projects were authorized and funded by Congress, on the other. In chapter 3, we discuss the development of the Carter administration's "veto strategy" that led to the most important veto of his presidency, as well as efforts by the administration and the president to sustain the veto. In chapter 4, we use quantitative data to examine the degree of presidential influence in Congress, especially in the face of countervailing influence wielded by members of Congress who opposed the president. In chapter 5, we turn to a discussion of our findings: the impact of the Carter administration on environmental and fiscal policy, how the veto foreshadowed the politics of the 1980s and beyond, and the governing lessons to be learned from this series of events.

CHAPTER 1

THE VETO AND PRESIDENTIAL INFLUENCE

Every Order, Resolution, or Vote to which the Concur-
rence of the Senate and House of Representatives may
be necessary (except on a question of Adjournment)
shall be presented to the President of the United States;
and before the Same shall take Effect, shall be approved
by him, or being disapproved by him, shall be repassed
by two thirds of the Senate and House of Representatives,
according to the Rules and Limitations prescribed in the
Case of a Bill.

—The Constitution of the United States,
Article 1, Section 8

The Constitution provides the president of the United States with
a limited hand in the legislative process. It grants the president

the power to veto legislation passed in the House and the Senate. This veto is sometimes referred to as a *negative power* because it allows the president to simply attempt to *stop* a bill from becoming a law; it does not provide the executive branch of government with the *positive power* to directly shape legislation other than by causing Congress to reconsider legislation and then resubmit repassed legislation that meets the president's concerns. Thus, the veto is mostly a blunt-force power that provides presidents with a take-it-or-leave-it option: either accept the bill and sign it, or veto it and allow Congress to attempt to invoke its constitutional power to override the president's veto with a two-thirds vote in both the House and Senate.

Despite the Founding Fathers' suspicion of strong executive power, the veto power was granted to the president to counteract attempts by Congress to encroach on executive power, and to stop any ill-conceived, unjust, or unconstitutional legislation that might be passed by Congress. Indeed, the fact that the representational basis of Congress is necessarily narrow and focused on small geographic districts and states might cause legislation to be insufficiently responsive to the "public good," and the veto would allow the president an opportunity to check the "institutional pathologies to which Congress is particularly susceptible" (Cameron 2000, 17), that is, the tendency to favor parochial interests over the national interest. From this perspective, the president is conceived of as a necessary bulwark in the U.S. system, one focused on the "common good," whose use of the veto is meant to restrain congressional weaknesses. James Bryce expressed this somewhat heroic view of the president's role in the political system (and the dismal role of Congress) in this way:

> The nation, which has often good grounds for distrusting Congress, a body liable to be moved by sinister private

influences, or to defer to the clamor of some noisy section outside, looks to the man of its choice to keep Congress in order. (quoted in Cameron 2000, 17)

In this chapter, we provide a broad overview of the veto politics literature, as well as the literature on presidential influence in Congress. Rather than provide an exhaustive review of these vast literatures, our purpose is to provide (1) sufficient background for understanding the nature of the relationship between the branches, and (2) perspectives on presidential influence. As such, our discussion is sufficiently cursory and meant to aid in understanding the empirical chapters that follow.

VETO POLITICS

Vetoing or signing a bill are not the only courses of action open to a president—presidents may also *threaten* to veto legislation.[1] In some respects, a veto threat is an attractive option for presidents: it imposes few short-term costs on presidents (talk is cheap), and a veto threat can positively influence (from the president's perspective) congressional action by invoking an "anticipated response" on the part of Congress. Under the

---

[1] Much of the literature on the veto focuses on the circumstances under which presidents exercise the veto power (see, for instance, Copeland 1983; Hoff 1991; Lee 1975; Rohde and Simon 1985). Using annual veto counts, the primary explanatory variables are composed of factors that lie outside of presidential control (party control of Congress, rate of unemployment, year within term, etc.). Focusing on individual bills, Gilmour (2002) argued that, controlling for external events, individual presidents develop different veto behaviors; the individual policy and strategic choices of presidents play an important role in whether the veto is exercised. Because our focus is presidential influence, we do not provide an exhaustive review of this related, but somewhat tangential, literature.

threat of a veto, Congress may craft legislation that is more consistent with the policy preferences of the president; in this case, Congress accepts half a loaf. If, however, Congress "calls the president's bluff" by passing legislation in the face of the veto threat, there are two possible outcomes. First, the president may tacitly acknowledge the bluff and sign the legislation—in this case, Congress is better off for ignoring the president's veto threat and passing legislation that is advantageous to its members. The cost to the president in this situation is to his future bargaining position; future veto threats may not be taken as seriously based on past unwillingness to carry through on a previous veto threat. Second, the president may choose to veto the legislation; however, vetoes impose costs on presidents: faced with the possibility of an override, a president must often dedicate many staff members and make his own efforts to avoid a successful override—resources that might be useful for influencing or passing legislation in which the president has an interest.

Considered from the point of view of Congress, a veto threat may be met with compromise legislation (i.e., legislation that is the product of compromise between actors) or by a failure to compromise the congressional position. Should the president exercise the veto, Congress may be faced with the difficult and costly task of securing an override. A successful override requires an extraordinary two-thirds majority in both chambers. Those familiar with the legislative process know that crafting a simple majority in favor of substantive legislation in both chambers is difficult; a two-thirds majority, then, is extraordinarily difficult. Furthermore, in attempting to override a veto, members of Congress and its leadership must invest their resources in lobbying on both sides of the override issue. Some members of Congress will need to invest their time and efforts in the override at the cost of pursuing other legislative goals; Congress will have to invest some significant time resources in debating and voting on the override, precious floor time that could be used for other legislative business.

Each side in the veto struggle has limited information about the policy preferences and political intentions of the other.[2] Questions abound on all sides. *For the president*: Is Congress willing to compromise or will they hold fast? Do my congressional adversaries have the votes necessary to override my veto? *For Congress*: Is the president likely to follow through and veto the bill as written? How much would have to change in the bill to avoid a presidential veto? *For the override advocates*: Can the necessary votes be marshaled to override the president's veto? *On all sides*: How will the public (House and Senate constituencies, and national constituencies) respond to all of this? Who will benefit and who will lose in a veto struggle? Is it worth it? In short, all sides in a veto struggle operate in an environment of "imperfect information."

Levels of information on both sides are sensitive to several contextual considerations. Whether there is one-party control of both Congress and the White House (united government) or split-party control of these institutions (divided government) is an important contextual factor. As Charles Cameron (2000) demonstrated, vetoes, especially those likely to involve extended rounds of veto bargaining, are more common during periods of divided government. One of the likely reasons for this (beyond

---

[2] Conley and Kreppel argued that veto situations are "one of the few real world examples of near-perfect information for all of the actors involved" because the vote tally on a conference report is public information, and "[t]he president has a very good idea of the potential success of a veto long before a veto is cast" (2001, 832). When we queried one interviewee about this, he responded, "No. You never know until the votes are counted" (Jim Free, interview with the authors, August 2007, Washington, DC).

considerations like substantive policy differences or political gamesmanship) is that information about policy preferences and political intentions are limited under divided government; presidents and the majority leadership in Congress are less likely to interact with one another and exchange information that would improve each side's ability to accurately determine the likely reaction of the other side during a veto bargaining process. Under united government, by contrast, information will flow more freely between the branches, thereby reducing, but not eliminating, uncertainty. Even under united government, however, the possibility of miscommunication, misperception, and obfuscation persists.

Congress considers a president of its own party differently than a president from the opposition party. Congress will be more hesitant to send a president of its own party legislation that will force him to make a difficult decision; such an action does not serve either actor well as it may raise issues about the party's ability to govern. Challenging a president of the governing party with a veto override will be rarer yet as it simply magnifies the incapacity of the ruling party. On the other hand, Congress may challenge a president of the opposition party by daring him to veto legislation and betting that the president will draw more ire from the public than will Congress. Continuing the battle by pursuing an override will simply add to perception of the president as intransigent or weak, which is exactly what the congressional party is attempting to create. Cameron's (2000, esp. 46–49) findings supported all three conjectures: vetoes are rarer in united government than in divided government, challenges of vetoes under united government are rare, and extended veto bargaining is more common under divided government.

Political time also plays a role in the level of uncertainty about the policy preferences on either side of the veto struggle, as discussed previously. Uncertainty abounds early in a president's term. A newly elected president faces initial challenges like having his cabinet members confirmed, gaining control over the bureaucracy, and proposing a revised budget. Regardless of past experience, a new president will not likely have a well-developed "veto strategy" that can be invoked upon his first congressional challenge; a president may well not know when he might issue a veto threat, much less choose to execute a veto. And the president's veto strategy is nested within the presence of united or divided government. Congress, facing a president with which it has no past experience, has no context for judging the credibility of a veto threat; only repeated interaction with a president will demonstrate a president's willingness to deliver on a veto threat.

Each side develops its veto strategy within the context of public opinion. Presidents appear to be more willing to threaten and exercise vetoes—and fight off overrides—when they enjoy high levels of public opinion.[3] The effect of a veto, or a veto threat, on a president's popularity is less clear. While James Bryce conjectured that "a president generally gains popularity by the bold use of his veto power" (quoted in Cameron 2000, 17), the theoretical and empirical literature suggest that a president's popularity is undermined by public bargaining with Congress over public policy (Cameron, Lapinski, and Reimann 2000; Groseclose and McCarty 2001; Matthews 1989). Groseclose and McCarty's theoretical model suggested that Congress puts forward legislation that will cause a president to use his vetoes in a way that makes the president appear extreme in the eyes of the public. In fact, according to their analysis, other things being

---

[3] See Deen and Arnold (2002) for a review of this literature.

equal, a veto of a major piece of legislation results in a drop in presidential approval of about two percentage points.

PRESIDENTIAL INFLUENCE

In Richard Neustadt's classic formulation, presidential influence in Congress is a function of a president's prestige outside the beltway—his standing in the public, that is, his job approval—and his reputation inside Washington (1954, 1990). His public standing is particularly important, Neustadt argued, because members of Congress will be less sanguine about casting a vote against a popular president. Taking into account their own interest in being reelected, members will not want to offend their constituents by being seen as obstructing the legislative agenda of a popular president. The president's reputation in Washington also plays a role in Congress. In particular, a veto threat is only as effective as it is credible; if Congress views a veto threat as hollow, they will react by ignoring it. Members may also gauge a president's willingness to follow through on threats of retaliation for voting against him. For instance, Lyndon Johnson developed a reputation as a president whom members did not want to find themselves in opposition to very often.

George Edwards (1989) built on Neustadt's conception of presidential leadership by suggesting that presidential influence exists "at the margins."[4] Relying on the concept of "anticipated response" developed by Neustadt, Edwards argued that most presidential influence is premised on members' expectations about how a vote in favor of, or against, a presidential position will be received in their constituency, and how it might impact

---

[4] See also Edwards' classic study, "Presidential Influence in the House" (1976).

their policy interests. In addition, Edwards argued, presidential influence increases as the president can build public support for particular policies:

> The likelihood that the president will obtain congressional support for his policies increases considerably if the president stands high in the polls and members of Congress either are concerned with how voters evaluate their support of the White House or use presidential approval ratings as indicators of public opinion. Support will also become more likely if the president's appeals for support are effectively made, the public is receptive to these requests, and the public communicates its support for the president to Congress. (1989, 219)

Edwards[5] used measures of presidential success (box scores) and found a relationship between public approval and support for the president on floor votes. This correlation between approval and support was cited as supportive of the Neustadt hypothesis. However, presidential power is an individual-level concept, that is, the president exercises influence over individual members of Congress, not over the institution as a whole. In fact, Edwards' hypothesis—that presidents exercise influence at the margins—explicitly suggested that presidential influence is only observable among a subset of individual members of Congress. When using aggregate measures, the research confuses units of analysis (using aggregate measures to make individual-level inferences); when using individual-level data, the analyses fail to define the subset of members that the president sought to influence. In sum, Edwards' correlations only hint at the likelihood of presidential influence.

---

[5] See, for instance, Edwards (1976, 1989).

Samuel Kernell further developed the concept of presidential influence in his classic work, *Going Public* (1997). For most of the history of the presidency, messages aimed at the public were mediated by the press. The advent of new technologies, however—first radio, then television, the subsequent profusion of outlets created by cable television, and more recently the Internet—allowed presidents to speak more directly to the American public, thus diminishing the mediating role of the Washington press corps. For Kernell (1997, ix),

> Going public is a class of activities that presidents engage in as they promote themselves and their policies before the American public...[it is] intended principally to place the president and his messages before the American people in a way that enhances his chances of success in Washington.

The primary focus of any president's public strategy is to build public support for the president's policies so that members of Congress find it difficult to oppose the president. Kernell provided evidence that suggests that direct appeals by the president to the public increased dramatically over the last century both in terms of presidential messages and in terms of presidential travel, all of which is aimed at influencing local and regional opinion that, in turn, will sway some members of Congress to support the president's position.

All of these works focused on behaviors and measures that are reasonably easy to observe and measure. Box scores provide easy access to information about who "wins" in Congress, roll call votes indicate who supported the president and who did not, and surveys of public opinion can routinely deliver measures of public support for the president. Moreover, it is easy to count presidential messages, press conferences, and trips. Simple correlations provide some hints about the relationship between the president and his standing with the public, but provide little leverage on the question of whether presidents are able to influence the votes of *individual* members of Congress. These measures provide some limited insight into the context within which members calculate their support for the president—and that is a large part of building supportive coalitions in Congress—but they cannot tell us how presidents influence those crucial votes that mean the difference between winning and losing.

Terry Sullivan's work sought to estimate presidential influence in Congress by looking at those votes in which the president had an active interest in order to determine whether presidents can "change minds" in Congress. He assumed White House "interest" in the outcome of a vote through the existence of White House headcounts of congressional support (Sullivan 1990, 1991a, 1991b, 2001). Unlike previous attempts to gauge presidential influence, Sullivan's work focused on the less easily observable process of influencing individual members' votes. Sullivan compared the initial positions of members of Congress with the positions taken on the final headcount conducted by the White House (mostly using headcounts from the Johnson administration) to estimate the degree to which White House interest shifted votes toward the president's position. His findings suggested that presidents were able to change the positions of members of Congress from opposition to support of the president's position, even in the face of considerable opposition.

Sullivan's approach is important for its use of archival sources and its effort to measure influence through changes in members' voting dispositions. His approach is also innovative. His focus on changes of position, in particular, is a vast improvement over simply observing the roll call behavior of members of Congress. Sullivan's focus on the presence of a headcount as a measure of exertion of presidential influence in Congress, however, is problematic. As Edwards argued, Sullivan has "no measure of *presidential involvement* (except that a headcount was taken). Thus…it is difficult to draw inferences about influence. We cannot attribute whatever changes do take place *to the president*" (1991, 726; emphasis added). To better understand presidential influence in Congress, it is critical to focus on direct presidential lobbying of members of Congress, and on a president's success or failure to convert members of Congress to support for the president's position. Sullivan's approach is also problematic in that it lumps together all votes; he did not make a distinction between votes where the White House invested considerable resources and those votes about which they simply wanted to be assured that they would win. All issues are not created equally. In particular, the critical resource of presidential effort will not be expended in all attempts to influence Congress. This suggests, then, that any attempt to estimate presidential influence ought to focus on those legislative battles for which *direct presidential lobbying* was employed.[6]

Regardless of potential shortcomings in past research, the general consensus in the literature is that *presidents matter*. Individual presidents are able to, and do, exercise influence in Congress by changing minds and changing votes. By focusing our attention on an important series of events, centered on a high-profile

---

[6] A similar critique applies to Conley and Kreppel's study of veto overrides (2001). They examine the behavior of vote-switchers on override votes, that is, those who switch from a position opposed to the president to a position supportive of the president on veto overrides. They claimed to find different switching behavior based on the type of veto (partisan, contested, or position-taking). However, their approach did not control for other causal factors or allow inferences about the role of presidential influence in the vote-switching behavior.

veto, in which the Carter administration risked its prestige and invested considerable resources, we expect to be able to definitively identify whether a president is, in fact, able to exercise influence in Congress. This "critical case" offers the opportunity to test one of the well-accepted conjectures in practical politics, and one of the most widely accepted theories in American politics. Our archival data allow us to more directly examine the role of presidential influence. President Carter *directly lobbied* dozens of House members leading up to the override, and we have access to his handwritten notes relating to those phone calls. Thus, we are able to identify those members who received a direct plea from the president to support his position and who subsequently switched their votes to support the president. Short of a personal confession from each such member that the president caused them to change their vote, this is the best available means of establishing that presidential influence led members to change their votes.

CHAPTER 2

MR. CARTER GOES TO WASHINGTON

President Carter really believed in it. He thought it was a waste of public money. We predicted what the outcome would be and he said "I'm going to do it anyway." I think we maybe underestimated it and certainly other people underestimated it. It caused a bitterness that took a long time to get over.

—Frank Moore[1]

---

[1] *Interview with Frank Moore (including William Cable, Dan Tate, and Robert Thompson)*, Miller Center for Public Affairs Presidential Oral History Program, September 18–19, 1981, 155.

President Jimmy Carter, initially almost alone, recognized that if the Democratic Party was to retain the loyalty of the American people and remain the majority party at the presidential level during the conservative period, it needed to move into a post-New Deal era while still retaining the best of the party's traditions. Much of the domestic side of the Carter presidency can be seen in the struggle to accomplish this result while retaining the loyalty of the liberal elements of the Party that cling to the government activism of FDR's New Deal and LBJ's Great Society. Far from being a traitor to his party, as some on the left insinuated, he realized that only by changing the party could he save it. The tragedy is that he did not have the chance to finish the job.

—Stuart Eizenstat[2]

The late Nelson Polsby, one of the foremost observers of Congress during the past fifty years, wrote the following about Jimmy Carter's relationship with Congress:

> Carter presented…a problem because he and his aides had run against Washington and had a disdain for Congress and because he ran a highly ineffective legislative liaison operation that dovetailed badly with whatever help he might receive from the newly empowered Speaker. (2004, 111)

Stephen Wayne offered a similar assessment of Carter's legislative effectiveness:

> Jimmy Carter was not a very effective legislator. This perception, shaped by memories of Lyndon Johnson and expectations of Democratic leadership, was shared by Congress and the public alike. The White House congressional liaison office took much of the blame for Carter's difficulties. (1982, 47)

---

[2] Interview with the authors, Washington, DC, August 2007.

Eric Davis (1979, 1983) is perhaps the scholar who most closely examined the operation of the Congressional Liaison Office during the Carter presidency, and his conclusions are consistent with those of Polsby and Wayne:

> Carter did achieve some legislative successes during his presidency…It often seemed, however, as if these successes were attained in spite of the work of the legislative liaison staff, not because of it. More importantly, Carter suffered a number of major defeats on Capitol Hill…A more politically skilled liaison staff might have been able to prevent these defeats, by keeping Democratic members of Congress in line behind the president's program and picking up Republican support for those programs where possible. (1983, 65–66)[3]

There is a nearly universal perception that Carter was a failure as a legislative leader, and that the Congressional Liaison Office headed by Frank Moore was, to some degree, responsible for this failure. Moore and his staff are often depicted as inexperienced and incompetent—the often repeated charge that Moore did not return the phone calls of members of Congress is ubiquitous and symbolic of a lack of political sophistication and proper respect for the institutional role of Congress.[4] Jimmy Carter is frequently blamed for not getting to know key members

---

[3] It should be noted that Davis based many of his conclusions on interviews conducted during the first year of the Carter administration. Members of the congressional liaison staff under Carter universally point to a big improvement in the operations of their office after that first year.

[4] Frank Moore maintains that this reputation for not returning phone calls stems from the period prior to Carter taking office, especially during the campaign when Moore viewed his position as one of coordinating joint campaign activities between Carter and Congress, and members of Congress, including congressional leaders and aides, were seeking him out on legislative matters. In addition, Moore points to the overwhelming number of phone calls that came in from Capitol Hill during the transition period, a period during which

of Congress, for not socializing with legislators as his predecessors had, and for not understanding the political consequences of his actions. Contemporary media accounts, combined with the memoirs of congressional leaders (particularly Tip O'Neill's biting account), solidify the view of an inept staff and a failed legislative leader. According to the conventional wisdom, if only Carter had been more like Lyndon Johnson, and Frank Moore had been more like Max Friedersdorf (Reagan's liaison), the Carter legacy would be one of success and not failure.

In our view, the impact of the perceived failings of the Liaison Office, and Carter's own persuasive difficulties, has been dramatically overstated. As Bond and Fleisher (1994, 287) pointed out, "[T]he perceptions of the Carter administration's relations with Congress were formed early in the term and, once formed, were slow to change regardless of the ensuing record." Instead, a more thorough evaluation of the contextual and policy factors that confronted the Carter administration indicates that regardless of the interpersonal relationships and skill of the Liaison Office (or Carter, for that matter), it would have been very difficult for any president to have had greater success than Carter experienced given his legislative goals and the nature of the times.[5] Many of the problems attributed to the president and his liaison staff can alternatively be viewed as the result of a Democratic congressional leadership hardened for a fight by eight years of battling the Nixon and Ford administrations, and unwilling to follow the president in policies that pulled

Moore did not know that he would be asked by Carter to serve as legislative liaison and during which there was virtually no congressional liaison staff.

[5] This was a politically and socially tumultuous time for the United States—the time of post-Vietnam, post-Watergate, and a post-reform Congress. These are just a few of the challenges that faced Carter as president; these issues would have faced anyone elected in 1976.

against the liberal pressures that had been sweeping the Caucus for years. Other contextual factors lessened the likelihood that Jimmy Carter would have an easy time dealing with Congress.

In this chapter, we discuss the contextual factors that Jimmy Carter confronted in his particular battle against water project spending and which pulled against presidential influence over Congress. For our purposes, these contextual factors may be divided into three broad categories, each of which will be discussed in turn: (1) the nature and history of water policy making in the United States, (2) the "outsider" framework of the Carter presidency in both its electoral and governing manifestations, and (3) the institutional and political congressional environment of change and reform that Carter encountered.

WATER SUBSYSTEMS POLITICS

The history of water policy in the United States can best be understood in the context of subsystem politics. Political scientists have focused considerable attention on the close relationship that often develops between interest groups, bureaucratic agencies, and members of congressional committees within specific policy areas. Whether described as "iron triangles," "subgovernments," "whirlpools," or "issue networks," scholars have argued that these relationships create strong pressures within the political system for policies favoring the narrow shared interests of the involved interest groups, agencies, and members of Congress, frequently at the expense of the public interest.[6] Perhaps no policy area has so often been characterized

---

[6] For a review of the literature on subsystems and a critique, see McCool (1998). For present purposes, we will use the term "subsystem" to apply to the interrelated groups involved in making water policy.

as fitting within this subsystem model as water policy making in the United States. And from the very beginnings of American government, opponents of federal spending on water projects have opposed the water subsystems with the claim that water policy subverts the national interest for the economic, electoral, and career interests of those within the subsystem who benefit from water project construction.

Critics of federal water policy first applied the pejorative term "pork barrel" to describe the behavior of Congress regarding the annual River and Harbor appropriation (Safire 1993). In 1879, *The New York Times* editorialized against water policy making and the water subsystem in the following strong language:

> Its supporters are bound together by the cohesive power of the public plunder...The support of the great bill is almost unanimous. No matter what else may fail, or what important public measure may be killed for want of time, the River and Harbor Appropriation Bill always goes through without debate, under suspension of the rules if necessary, but it goes through, because every member sees in it a chance to distribute the public money among his constituents...It is the outcome of a vicious practice which is increasing year by year. It is not only an extravagance which merits the severest denunciation, but it has taken the form of a raid upon the public Treasury, which is not much better than downright robbery.

For as long as presidents and outsiders in the media have ridiculed water project spending as a wasteful "pork barrel," members of Congress, along with their allies in the interest groups and the federal water agencies, have staunchly defended the practice, and have viewed attacks against water projects as attacks on their very honor and their institutional independence. In 1896 Louisiana senator Joseph E. Ransdell (1916, 45) publicly defended water policy in the *Annals of the American Academy of Political Science*:

> The committees of Congress did their utmost to enact laws in regard to rivers and harbors that were fair, just, and beneficial to the public at large, regardless of individual Congressmen or private interest...fewer errors were made in the preparation and passage of river and harbor bills than in any class of legislation enacted by Congress. I deny with all the force of my being that there was any real "pork" in the river and harbor bills passed by Congress during the past fifteen years, and defy anyone to prove the contrary.

Despite the claims of key members of Congress to the contrary, the most exhaustive political science study of water projects (Ferejohn 1974) found considerable evidence that one water agency in particular, the Army Corps of Engineers, had a special relationship with Congress and key committee members in the budgetary arena. Ferejohn found that the Army Corps received other advantages as well (a very low discount rate on cost benefit analyses, for example) due to congressional support. Ferejohn concluded that "the principal institutional features leading to overspending in public works are those that constitute the very basis of representative government as it exists in the United States: Geographic representation, majority rule, and the committee system" (252). Moreover, he argued that the push for public works spending in general, and water project spending in particular, was rooted in the Madisonian system enshrined in the U.S. Constitution and in the institutionalization of the modern Congress. According to Ferejohn:

> Water projects in particular are something that congressmen generally believe can help them get reelected.

> Basically, the process can work in two ways. In the first place, getting the projects can be symbolically important in a reelection campaign, since it shows voters that their congressman can do things for them in Washington... Perhaps even more important is the fact that projects provide benefits for a few well-organized groups in the district. Construction workers, contractors, and local businessmen receive economic rewards from nearly any sort of construction project: these groups frequently contain important potential contributors to, or workers in, a particular congressman's campaign. (1974, 49)[7]

Former presidential adviser to Franklin Roosevelt and Secretary of the Interior Harold Ickes, who had a close up view of how the water subsystem worked, used the following language to describe the operation of the water subsystem:

> The amazing American phenomenon, the pork barrel, emerged in complete and functioning order from the teeming Corps of Army Engineers. The theory behind it is that the harder the people scratch to pay their taxes, the more money there will be for the Corps of Army Engineers to scratch out of the Treasury with the aid of Congress in order to maintain its control of that body by building, more or less justifiable or downright unjustifiable projects in the various states and districts for which senators and representatives may claim credit during the next election campaign. What matters if many of these projects are against the wishes of, or even in defiance of orders from, the President himself? An

---

[7] Ferejohn also pointed out that members of Congress viewed the provision of water projects as a way to buy political capital with local constituencies in order to allow them the freedom to vote against the feeling of the constituency on other issues of importance to the national party establishment.

Army Corps' "Operation Santa Claus" is a two-pronged affair—the Engineers lobbying directly for an appropriation by the Congress while inciting local constituencies to bring pressure to bear on their senators and representatives. (Maass 1951, xi)

It was into this most difficult policy arena—where Congress had historically jealously guarded its power to dictate policy in cooperation with powerful bureaus and closely allied interests groups, and where presidents tried to gain influence and failed—that Jimmy Carter sought to make his first major effort to control congressional spending. Miller (1984, 285–286) pointed out that Carter's predecessors and the Office of Management and Budget (OMB) had prepared lists identifying water projects for elimination for more than forty years, but no administration (including those of Nixon and Ford) had "dared move beyond the planning stages." Carter had been clear during his campaign that water projects would be an early target to reduce federal spending (Bonafede 1977). However, Congress' love affair with water projects had been going on for well over a century when Jimmy Carter stepped into the White House. Water projects had a symbolic importance that may have even overshadowed the dollars that were to be spent in the congressional districts and states. They had been part of the tug of war between president and Congress for years, and within one month of taking office, Jimmy Carter decided to challenge a Congress that only recently had reasserted itself in doing battle with Richard Nixon and Gerald Ford. Carter's willingness, even eagerness, to take on the powerful water policy subsystems can only be understood through the lens of his outsider perspective. It is to a discussion of the anti-Washington character of Carter's election and administration that we now turn.

THE OUTSIDER: THE 1976 ELECTION

Vietnam, Watergate, the Nixon resignation, and Gerald Ford's pardon of Richard Nixon had all contributed to anti-government sentiments among the American electorate. The public seemed sick and tired of Washington politics and Jimmy Carter, the former governor of Georgia, offered an alternative. He was an "outsider," never having served in elective office in Washington. While his status as an outsider would serve him well in the general election, it was not necessarily a virtue in the pursuit of the Democratic nomination. Less well-known than his competitors— Senator Henry Jackson (WA), Senator Lloyd Bentsen (TX), Senator Birch Bayh (IN), Senator Frank Church (ID), and Representative Mo Udall (AZ), to name a few—Carter performed surprisingly well in the Iowa Caucuses, establishing early momentum, which carried him to the Democratic nomination.

In the general election, Carter's status as an outsider benefited him. Incumbent President Gerald Ford had been roundly criticized for his pardon of Richard Nixon for his role in Watergate; combined with a primary challenge by Ronald Reagan, economic stagnation, and characterizations of Ford as non-presidential and clumsy, Ford was not a particularly strong candidate. Congressional Democrats were especially critical of Ford's liberal use of the veto power. Carter used his outsider status to attack Washington, and Congress in particular, as composed of profligate politicians who have only their own electoral fortunes in mind. He positioned himself and the presidency as a cure for directing Congress toward policies that benefit the entire nation. Adopting a Wilsonian approach to the presidency, Carter cast himself as a "trustee" president who would choose what was right for the public good over parochial interests (Jones 1988).

After amassing a 30 percent point lead in early polls, Carter narrowly won the presidency and evidenced no coattails, bringing with him only one additional Democrat to the House and one to the Senate. Carter carried only 220 of 435 congressional districts, and ran ahead of the congressional Democratic candidates in only twenty-two districts (Ornstein 1981, 91). As it was portrayed, this was no landslide, and there was not a single member of Congress who owed their job to the new president; it was an inauspicious beginning, and Carter's anti-politics and anti-politician rhetoric, which played so well in the electorate, did not resonate as well in Congress. Carter's view of politics was consistent with the heroic analyses of the presidency promoted by academics like James Bryce and Woodrow Wilson: it was the president's responsibility to check the narrow-minded and spendthrift habits of a Congress.

A conservative Democrat, Carter was the first southerner elected president since Reconstruction (Johnson won as an incumbent president following Kennedy's assassination), and the last Democratic nominee to win the "solid South" (excepting Virginia). Perhaps lost during the campaign and its aftermath—the definition of the campaign as a repudiation of Nixon–Ford and the political resurgence of the South—was the fact that the Jimmy Carter campaign had promised to reduce the deficit by controlling spending:

> I had inherited the largest deficit in history—more than $66 billion—and it was important to me to stop the constantly escalating federal expenditures that tended to drive up interest rates and were one of the root causes of inflation and unemployment." (Carter 1995, 81)

The chief means of addressing the deficit, according to Carter, was eliminating "waste and pork barrel projects in the federal budget" (Carter 1995, 82).

Taking on the deficit by way of water projects in particular was consistent with Carter's progressive views on the environment. It was also attractive from a public relations perspective: environmental concerns were riding the wave of the first Earth Day seven years earlier, spawning many significant environmental policies; and axing water projects was popular as an extension of sentiments regarding environmental protection. And Carter staffed his administration with many environmentalists: former governor Cecil Andrus as Secretary of Interior, Andrus' Assistant Secretary of Interior Guy Martin, and former California state assemblyman Charles Warren as head of the Council on Environmental Quality; moreover, Katherine Fletcher, a scientist with the Environmental Defense Fund, worked under Stuart Eizenstat, head of the Domestic Policy Council. The Carter administration could thus be considered as one of the most pro-environmental in the history of the office (Stine 1998), and they quickly took aim at water projects (Reisner 1993; Stine 1998).

The issue of dams and other water projects melded Carter's fiscal conservatism and his environmental views. As governor of Georgia, he had engaged in a lengthy battle with the Army Corps of Engineers over the Sprewell Bluff Dam, which was to have been built on the Flint River. Although Carter initially supported the project, he subsequently studied the situation and came to the conclusion that the Army Corps of Engineers' analysis of the project was faulty and vetoed the project. His experience with the Spewrell Bluff Dam led Carter to believe that many other Corps projects were both economically inefficient, if not downright wasteful, as well as bad for the environment.[8] Bill

---

[8] On Carter and the Spewrell Bluff Dam, see Clymer (1977), Miller (1984), and Reisner (1993). In an interview with the authors, Carter's Deputy Press Secretary Rex Granum was particularly adamant that one cannot understand

Cable, a member of the congressional liaison team, summarized the intersection between Jimmy Carter's budget policy agenda and Congress' interest in perpetuating the water projects:

> The President decided that a national water policy had to be considered in terms of where public money was spent. Water projects tended to be given to those people that had the most ability to affect the system within the Congress without regard to, and almost in spite of, Presidential review. The President did promise to be different. Most of the guys in Washington who were the most bitter, either didn't believe it when he was campaigning on it, didn't hear it, or didn't want to hear it. When he did do it, they blamed him for doing it. They resented him for it. Some of the people that are considered as Jimmy Carter's friends and supporters in the Congress resented the hell out of the President for publicly raising an issue about the way they spend money, for the way they conducted the public's business. People didn't like it. People described the President as having some sort of feeling toward the Congress that they were all a little bit dirty or tainted or somehow or another less good or less clean.[9]

In taking on this issue, Carter was taking on one of the sacred cows of congressional politics, though he was doing so in a way that was consistent with his understanding of the presidency.[10]

Carter's move against the water projects without an understanding of Carter's experience with the Flint River and the Spewrell Bluff Dam in Georgia.

[9] *Interview with Frank Moore (including William Cable, Dan Tate, and Robert Thompson)*, Miller Center for Public Affairs Presidential Oral History Program, September 18–19, 1981, 16.

[10] Using more poetic, if somewhat hyperbolic, language, Reisner described water projects as "the grease gun that lubricates the nation's legislative machinery. Congress without water projects would be like an engine without oil; it would simply seize up" (1993, 308).

Pork barrel projects highlight a general tension between Congress and the president over the power of the purse. It is true that money cannot be spent from the public treasury without the approval of Congress, but presidents have done battle with Congress as they attempted to gain control over federal spending using their budgeting powers: the power to propose the budget, impoundment of funds (ruled unconstitutional during the Nixon presidency), deferral of spending, and proposed rescissions. Presidents often claim to represent "the interests of the nation" in promoting projects that serve the "greater good"—often criticizing the parochial nature of congressional spending priorities—but members of Congress chafe at the idea that the executive branch lays claim to knowing what is best for their constituencies. Majority Leader Jim Wright (D-TX), a longtime member of the Public Works Committee, took umbrage at the Carter administration's hostility toward these projects. As Frank Moore said:

> You'd say [to Wright] "we don't need to spend two million dollars on this dam for a study of so-and-so," and his reply was "who knows better what is needed for the district than the congressman who represents that district? Certainly they know better what the people in a district want than a bunch of people in the White House; a bunch of punk pencil pushers at OMB."[11]

---

[11] *Oral History Interview with Frank Moore*, Jimmy Carter Library and Museum, July 30–31, 2002, 108. It should be pointed out that Majority Leader Wright had used his position on the Public Works Committee to assist other members in obtaining projects, and this was at least partially responsible for Wright's selection as majority leader. When asked whether he thought that his position on Public Works helped him get elected, Majority Leader Wright told the authors:

> Well, probably so. I was on Public Works for twenty years and I was in the position to support the legislation that was beneficial to a lot of

Carter's identification of deficits as part of a culture of corruption in Washington is consistent with an ongoing theme in American politics tracing back to the founding of the American Republic, but it was counter to the policies adopted by the Democratic Party since the New Deal and put Carter in the position of portraying his congressional allies, who had presided over the deficit that Carter inherited, as somehow corrupt (Savage 1988). In September 1976 candidate Carter tried to lay the blame for the federal deficit on President Ford and the Republicans:

> The Republicans say they are the party of fiscal responsibility. But their record shows the worst fiscal mismanagement in our history...The deficit for the year just ended is $65 billion. This is the largest deficit in our history. It is larger than the deficits of all eight Kennedy–Johnson years combined.

It was a Democratic Congress, however, that was the driving force behind many of the programs Carter wished to cut. But deficits were not only morally wrong in the president's estimation: Carter made an explicit link between federal deficits and *inflation* during the campaign, and continued to emphasize this link

---

different people. There were these omnibus bills, omnibus rivers and harbors bills every two or every three years. We would pass a bill that would authorize projects, flood control projects, navigation projects, authorize the construction of Post Offices in the early days, things of that kind, and there were people, members who would come to you and want those things and my nature was to help them. Because if it was warranted I went along with it. People felt at least that I was a good guy I guess. (Interview with the authors, March 2001, Fort Worth, TX)

At this point, Wright was concerned about a potential challenge from Representative Phillip Burton (CA), either for majority leader or in the future for Speaker, and apparently felt that continued provision of water projects would be politically important.

(some might say overemphasize it) throughout his presidency.[12] In order to keep his campaign pledge to not lie to the American people, Carter would have to aggressively attack deficits, and in a climate that witnessed the spread of the Proposition 13 tax revolt that began in Californian in 1978, Carter's attack on deficits would need to be targeted at reducing spending rather than tax increases.

Carter encountered a congressional leadership that viewed deficit spending in a much different light. During the previous eight years, the Democratically controlled Congress had sparred with Presidents Nixon and Ford over the level of federal spending, and the new congressional leadership was more focused on meeting the pent-up demand for spending programs targeted at traditional Democratic constituencies than it was in reducing the federal deficit. Domestic Policy Adviser Stuart Eizenstat (1994, 6) summed up the differing perspectives in the following passage:

> Nothing better typified the difference between Jimmy Carter and the liberal wing of the Democratic Party which dominated Washington than an early conversation between the new president and the new Speaker, Tip O'Neill, at one of the first Democratic Leadership Breakfasts. The president told an incredulous Speaker that the "greatest albatross around the neck of the Democratic Party" was the perception of its fiscal irresponsibility. He told Tip he meant to reverse the normal relationship in which Democratic presidents tended to ask for more

---

[12] In hindsight, President Carter's repeated emphasis that the federal deficit was the driving force behind high levels of inflation was probably overblown. According to Savage (1988, 9–10): "By the end of Ronald Reagan's first term as president, most empirically based economists agreed that federal deficit spending during the preceding half-century produced primarily salutary, or at worst benign, effect in the economy."

spending from Congress than they got. Tip said that this is not what he had expected to hear after eight years of Republican presidents.

The Outsider: Transitioning to Power

In his study of presidential transitions, Charles O. Jones (1998, 34) pointed out the following:

> The fact that Jimmy Carter was an outsider, even within his own party, no doubt aided him immeasurably in winning the nomination in the first post-Watergate election. But that status was of little or no help in designing an effective transition.

In fact, being an outsider poses particular difficulties due to lack of experience in matters of governing and inherent suspicion from the Washington community. Carter's transition appears to have been especially problematic: Neustadt (1990, 239) said that the Carter administration was "particularly prone" to transition hazards.[13]

Much of the difficulty that Carter had in transitioning to become president has been subsequently attributed to two key items: (1) a desire to perpetuate the outsider philosophy of the campaign by relying more heavily on a circle of insiders who

---

[13] Neustadt claimed that Carter's decision to run his transition operation from Plains, Georgia, alienated the establishment press who would cover Carter during his four years in office. According to Neustadt (1990, 242): "In Plains there were few excitements except softball games, which he himself played grimly. He thus incurred the wrath of his assigned reporters (whose counterparts in 1960 had enjoyed more pleasures, better stories, and no grimness in Hyannis Port, Palm Beach, Georgetown and Manhattan). For much of this he was to pay high prices in due course." For an insider's account of the relations between the Carter administration and the press, see Powell (1984).

were close to Carter in Georgia as key White House staff, and (2) the lack of an overriding ideology or theme to guide the administration as it took over the reins of power in Washington. Many critics of Carter criticize the transition for failing to reach out more to the Washington community for advice and personnel. Hamilton Jordan, the Carter adviser given most credit for putting together the outsider campaign strategy when no one in the establishment believed that Jimmy Carter had a chance of securing the Democratic nomination, receives the most blame for creating an insular White House, allegedly disdaining the Washington establishment.[14]

Regardless of who is at fault for the poor interpersonal relationships that appeared during the transition and, subsequently (and there certainly is enough blame to go around), many of Carter's key lieutenants viewed the political environment as biased against Carter and the Georgians from day one. Jordan claims the following (2000, 65):

> By the time we arrived in Washington, there was a strong but subtle feeling: 'You guys from Georgia won the White House by running against Washington, through political gimmickry and just plain dumb luck...but we are going to show you who is Boss in this town!'

Both critics (Fallows 1977) and supporters (Jordan 1994) also point to the absence of an overriding governing purpose as a key

---

[14] There has been a large amount written about the relationship between Carter's key aides and the Washington establishment from both perspectives. See, for example, O'Neill and Novak (1987) for an establishment perspective, and Powell (1984) and Jordan (2000) for Carter administration perspectives. While the details of the social relationship are beyond the scope of the present study, the hard feelings engendered carry on to this day and, while difficult to measure, certainly did play a role, though secondary to the institutional factors discussed in this volume.

factor that hampered Carter's transition and did not foster a dedicated group of hard-core supporters. According to Jordan (1994,
165), "Probably most importantly—and here, this is no one's
fault but our own, we did not arrive in Washington with a unifying philosophy to pull the political considerations, problems,
needs, hopes, and aspirations of the American people together."

Frank Moore, who would serve as the presidential assistant
for congressional liaison throughout the Carter years, identified
two shortcomings of the transition that impeded the effectiveness
of congressional relations during the first months of the Carter
administration: the late development of a formal legislative
agenda, which then became too long with no unifying theme; and
the heavy reliance on cabinet government, which caused the
White House to become overly reliant on congressional relations staff from with the government departments. Moore, who
had been a Carter aide when the latter was governor of Georgia,
became the point man for congressional relations in the new
administration, though he had no experience dealing with Congress prior to the campaign. He had begun working on the Carter
campaign in a campaign finance role and subsequently segued
into the role of coordinating campaign activities between Carter
and congressional Democrats. Though he was not responsible
for coordinating legislative activities during the campaign period
(and through the transition), it was widely assumed that he was
Carter's link to Congress and therefore versed in the Georgian's
legislative goals. As he recalled:

> Again, we didn't have a legislative agenda. People asked,
> "What's your agenda going to be?" We didn't have one
> at that time. Our agenda was to get elected. We stayed
> away from issues in our campaign. Part of our campaign
> strategy was never talk about issues. The only time we
> ever did we got in trouble for it. The people said, "Well,

Carter's fuzzy on those issues." He sure as hell was. A [*sic*] so we didn't have a legislative program. People asked me about it. I said I don't know what we've got. They said, "Moore's dumb, he's supposed to be legislative liaison and he doesn't know what he is doing." People were developing agendas. People unknown to us at that time I suppose. I really wasn't doing congressional liaison, I was doing campaign coordination. We didn't care what bills were going on, we wanted to win the election. We had a flap with the Speaker early on the post card registration. We well knew that we didn't want to get involved in legislation at that time. When I took on the congressional liaison, we suggested CL be organized in this way. I didn't ask him for a job. I had never lobbied before. I don't even recall how I learned that I was going to be the White House congressional liaison person. It may have been down at Sea Island. The press probably forced it by asking who's the White House staff going to be. Hamilton and Jack Watson had a thing going on with them about who's going to be chief of staff at that time. Maybe when that was settled and they decided on who would head CL.[15]

During the transition period, Frank Moore spent much of his time escorting potential Carter nominees to interview with the president-elect in Plains, Georgia. Frank Moore did not learn that he would be presidential assistant for congressional liaison until "very close to January 20th (inauguration)."[16]

Carter had campaigned as an outsider and approached the transition from the outside as well. In governing, Carter also sought to shake up government, proposing a controversial reorganization

---

[15] *Interview with Frank Moore (including William Cable, Dan Tate, and Robert Thompson)*, Miller Center for Public Affairs Presidential Oral History Program, September 18–19, 1981, 14.
[16] Ibid.

initiative upon taking office that angered key House Committee Chair Jack Brooks immediately. However, the one prominent feature of his governing philosophy, which was a reflection of his outsider status and was an effort to break from the practice of Richard Nixon, and which had an impact on his relations with Congress, was the emphasis on cabinet government.

THE OUTSIDER: CABINET GOVERNMENT

Jimmy Carter came to Washington pledging cabinet government. He believed that his predecessors, Nixon in particular, had so centralized the power of government in the White House as to diminish its responsiveness to the American people. Carter believed that the agencies and bureaus of the federal bureaucracy were closest to the people and should be empowered to carry out the business of government. His belief in cabinet government influenced his relations with Congress, motivating an initial legislative liaison structure that delegated much responsibility to the cabinet departments and that led to a White House congressional liaison structure that did not facilitate working relationships between staffers and their targets of influence. Frank Moore claimed that the original structuring of the congressional liaison staff along issue rather than regional lines was dictated by Carter's belief in cabinet government:[17]

> The reason we had such a small staff to begin with is because President Carter originally felt he was dedicated to cabinet government. He asked, "Why have a big White House congressional liaison staff?" HEW had forty people

---

[17] *Interview with Frank Moore (including William Cable, Dan Tate, and Robert Thompson)*, Miller Center for Public Affairs Presidential Oral History Program, September 18–19, 1981, 14.

> in congressional liaison; the Defense Department had hundreds. Commerce maybe had thirty people…The smallest federal agencies, even NASA, had as big or bigger congressional liaison staffs than the White House. Our idea was to farm out the stuff; let them do it. What we were doing in the White House was to coordinate this. The reason that it didn't work was that every Senator and every Congressman first wants to talk to the President.

There was recognition among congressional liaison staff early on that this was problematic. Frederick T. "Rick" Merrill, who was initially chief House liaison but left the White House in May 1977, wrote an article that appeared soon after in *Washington Monthly* discussing the difficulty of relying so heavily on a department-centered model of congressional liaison, and when Bill Cable was brought on to be the new lead House liaison later in 1977, he endeavored to change the way that the House operation within congressional liaison was organized, with, according to him, only mixed success.[18] The problems associated with delegating so much responsibility to the departments and maintaining only a small White House staff are threefold: (1) as discussed previously, there is a tendency for government bureaus to collaborate with interest groups and congressional committees at the expense of the president's agenda; (2) under the original Carter organization, the White House staff were not in the position to trade favors across different policy areas, but were organized to deal with all members in certain, defined policy domains; and (3) members of Congress value the respect that is conveyed with contacts of a presidential nature (not departmental contacts) and resent the lack of White House involvement.

---

[18] *William H. Cable Exit Interview*, Presidential Papers Project, February 2, 1981.

It was widely known that the members of the Army Corps of Engineers are advocates for the projects that they build, and Jimmy Carter was well aware of the Corps' past behavior, having tangled with the Corps over the Sprewell Bluff Dam Project when he was governor of Georgia.[19] Yet according to the cabinet government model that was brought to the White House by Carter, the Army Corps would be in a key institutional position to defend the proposed water project cuts. As expected, the Army Corps of Engineers' lobbyists did not work in lock step with the White House as advocates to eliminate funding for Corps water project appropriations. In fact, administration officials pointed out that during the water wars, Army Corps of Engineers officials worked at cross-purposes with the White House:

> The Army Corps of Engineers guys on the water projects were up there [on Capitol Hill] and flat just 180° opposite of Presidential decision. You can get mad; you can't do anything about it. We tried to do something on a couple of those Corps of Engineers guys on water projects to the point where the President at one point spoke with the Secretary about what could be done. I don't know how you deal with it. It's going to go on forever. We did not deal with it as well in the beginning. I say "we." It was a decision the President made before I got there. In my view, President Carter overreacted to the excesses of the Nixon concentration of power in the White House. We went too far in Cabinet government. It was basically good, but you need some people in every department and

---

[19] The problems associated with relying on the Corps of Engineers to represent the president have continued into the administration of George W. Bush. In 2002 Mike Parker was asked to resign his position as assistant secretary over the Army Corps of Engineers on account of his statements criticizing the administration's budget proposals during congressional committee hearings; see Bumiller (2002).

agency who are beholden to Jimmy Carter and not either
to the program of the agency or the Secretary. I would
like a deputy as Under Secretary, a Deputy Secretary,
somebody at the top of that decision-making line in every
department and agency reviewing stuff that's going on
with the best interests of President Carter, or any President, in hand.[20]

Tip O'Neill (1987, 309) agreed, believing that some of Carter's
problems stemmed from his avoidance of political criteria and
loyalty in the appointments of those who worked in the departments of government. Not only was Carter struggling to overcome the historic pulls of the water policy subsystem, but also
he relied so heavily on the departments that were staffed without
consideration of political loyalty:

Many of the Carter appointees who came into federal
agencies acted as though they were hired strictly on merit,
and didn't owe anything to anybody. They refused to see
themselves as team players. I wasn't the only one who
had problems with them; not even Frank Moore could

---

[20] Bill Cable, *Interview with Frank Moore (including William Cable, Dan
Tate, and Robert Thompson)*, Miller Center for Public Affairs Presidential
Oral History Program, September 18–19, 1981, 36. Author Marc Reisner
(1993, 319–320) relayed the following anecdote: "Once, as (one of Carter's
House lobbyists) Jim Free was passing by the Public Works Committee room,
he noticed several high-ranking officers of the Corps talking with [commit-
tee chairman] Ray Roberts. Free stopped and eavesdropped long enough to
capture the gist of the conversation. They were laughing about how they were
going to beat us at our own game." Eizenstat (quoted in Miller 1984, 308)
stressed the information exchange between the Army Corps, the Bureau of
Reclamation, and their congressional committees as problematic: "one had the
sense as well that both agencies, that whatever was said, the members of Congress fairly quickly knew."

accomplish much with these people, who simply refused to follow his directives. (O'Neill and Novak, 309)

Based on the belief in cabinet government, the Office of Congressional Liaison was also organized in a way that did not allow it to take advantage of deals that could be struck across policy areas. Rick Merrill was openly critical of the impact that the issue-oriented structure was having on Carter's legislative relations. He claimed:

> When Carter took office, he wanted to eliminate the cynical horse-trading of the Nixon era and return some of the lobbying power to the departments...A White House liaison officer is no longer in a position to discuss a sewage treatment plant in the context of a foreign aid vote because the legislative aide who handles foreign policy does not also handle environmental issues—and besides, decisions on such matters no longer lie exclusively in the hands of the White House. (1977, 30)

Nixon's manipulation of the federal grant process was something that Carter wanted to avoid. He was so convinced that the merits of an argument were the essential factor in determining whether it would succeed or fail, that he consciously sought to avoid involvement in the quid pro quo that often characterizes politics. Several members of Carter's White House staff today admit that from time to time congressional votes were influenced through a promise of political favors; however, they universally contend that Carter himself did not engage in deal making, and he would stop an aide in mid-sentence who wished to discuss such deals.[21]

---

[21] One Carter aide told the authors the following: "I mean I went up with an official of the Office of Management and Budget and we went around and we were giving out bridges and federal buildings and at one point he said, 'I've

The following passage from Domestic Policy Adviser Eizenstat sums up Carter's view toward political deals:

> Jimmy Carter possesses...a belief in a sharp separation between the politics of campaigning and the politics of government; indeed, he disdained politics in governing as tawdry; would snap at advisers who suggested a course of action on political grounds; and at bottom, did not particularly like politicians or enjoy their company. To Carter, politics was a necessary evil to get elected in order to do "good" for the public at large.[22]

Jimmy Carter's predecessors had relied heavily on the federal grants process and the power to make patronage appointments to facilitate better relations with Congress. Carter's options and resources when he assumed the presidency were considerably less than those of his Democratic predecessors, and Carter's own moralistic outlook on the presidency made excessive use of these perquisites of office problematic, as Carter's reputation depended on avoiding charges of hypocrisy and dishonesty. Although Carter's congressional liaison did use the power of presidential spending from time to time to build coalitions, they were criticized by some for not making better use of presidential pork. According to Bill Cable:[23]

---

got to go back I've just run out of money'" (Interview with the authors, August 2007, Washington, DC). However, Carter refused to even discuss the deals that had been negotiated.

[22] Interview with the authors, August 2007, Washington, DC.

[23] *Interview with Frank Moore (including William Cable, Dan Tate, and Robert Thompson)*, Miller Center for Public Affairs Presidential Oral History Program, September 18–19, 1981; see also *William H. Cable Exit Interview*, Presidential Papers Project, February 2, 1981.

[Kennedy's and Johnson's legislative liaison] Larry O'Brien had a grant announcement operation that we got working late, but didn't initially have. He had one person who did nothing but sit on the telephone upstairs in what was Anne Wexler's office then. Congressional liaison had all the end of the second floor where Stu's office was. He had one person sit with a star set on so he could use both hands, and the grants came in from agencies he just sat and called all day long making grant announcements. They used those announcements, who was going to make them, who was going to notify them, whether the Senate or House got them and use them for rewards and maybe punishment. We didn't have that in there.

The amount of grant spending at the discretion of the executive branch had been curtailed in response to the excesses of the Nixon administration. Several grant programs—which had been established as categorical projects grants and were thus susceptible to political manipulation by the White House—and a grant-by-grant basis had been combined by Congress into block grants distributed by formulas in order to avoid the coercion that had been exerted by the Nixon White House.

The consolidation of a number of Great Society categorical project grant programs into the General Revenue Sharing Program, authorized by the State and Local Fiscal Assistance Act of 1972, reduced the grant-making discretion that could be concentrated in the White House. Two additional block grants, the Housing and Community Development Act of 1974 and the Comprehensive Employment and Training Act of 1973, were added during the Nixon years, further reducing potential presidential influence over grant making (Brown, Fossett, and Palmer 1984). Bill Cable, who had served as professional staff on the House Education and Labor Committee—which oversaw these changes in the structure and operation of grant programs—and later headed up the House liaison in the Carter White House, claimed that the changes in grant distribution method had an impact on Carter's ability to dole out grants for political purposes:[24]

> I think that an overreaction to the excesses of Haldeman and Ehrlichman kind of—the perception of Haldeman and Ehrlichman signing off on every federal grant that went out. I know that was impossible to do. There's no way that you can do it. As a matter of fact, the Congress spent most of the eight years that Richard Nixon was in the White House and the four years that Jimmy Carter was in the White House, eight from Nixon and Ford, limiting secretarial discretion. Basically, the discretion is very minimal, in one sense. The formula programs are written such that if an eligible recipient, be that a county or a city or a housing authority or a water authority or whatever, meets X prescribed criteria, 1-2-3-4-5, they're in the pool. And they get a proportionate share of the monies that are done. And the secretary really only exercises discretion in the terms of molding those applications into a form that fits the requirements of the statute. Because the Congress wanted to take away the ability of the President to manipulate that kind of thing. And we did it. We spent a long time writing that.

Carter's lack of direct White House involvement in grant issuance and announcement is now part of the common lore about the Carter administration. From the perspective of Congress, it is usually cited as emblematic of the failure of the White House to understand how politics in Washington had always worked. Tip O'Neill (1987, 308) frequently made the assertion that Carter

---

[24] *William H. Cable Exit Interview*, Presidential Papers Project, February 2, 1981.

worked against the electoral interests of Congress by not using the grants process more wisely:

> Once when the city of Boston applied for a government grant for some new roads, I called the Carter people to try to speed it along. Instead of assisting me, however, they did everything possible to block my way. When it came to helping out my district, I actually received more cooperation from Reagan's staff than from Carter's.

It wasn't just pork that was in short supply and disdained by the President. Patronage, the time-honored practice of rewarding your political allies with key government positions in Washington and in the regional offices, was both in short supply and looked down upon as somehow tawdry by Jimmy Carter. That there were considerably fewer slots available in the administration when Carter took office was partly due to the actions of the Ford administration in converting a number of previously political jobs into civil service jobs and then filling them with their former political occupants. In addition, as part of Carter's frugality and anti-Washington orientation, he came to office pledging to reduce the size of the White House staff, certainly a self-inflicted wound when it comes to patronage. Finally, and most importantly perhaps, was Carter's belief that appointments should be given to those most technically qualified and that cabinet secretaries should be allowed to select appointees from their own departments without much White House involvement.

But patronage was on the minds of members of Congress, especially during the first several meetings between the House Democratic leadership and high White House officials. During an early February meeting with Vice President Mondale, members freely shared their views regarding political appointments. Several months later, on June 14, 1977, patronage was again on the minds of members of Congress when the House leadership met with Hamilton Jordan, Frank Moore, and Jim King.[25] Just months into the Carter presidency, many members of Congress were furious over the slow pace of political appointments in the bureaucracy. Tip O'Neill began the meeting by complaining about the seemingly slow pace of administration action, and he concluded his opening salvo by zeroing in on the problem as he saw it: "We won an election but you'd never know it!" Hamilton Jordan's initial attempts to explain the difficulties faced by the White House, as well as his mantra that "we don't have too many jobs to fill," fell on deaf ears. Majority Leader Wright asked the question point blank: "What input does a member of Congress have on appointments? Of all my recommendations only one has gotten a job—and it was ceremonial." Whip John Brademas followed up, "[Y]ou don't even give interviews [to our recommendations] and I resent it." In the meantime, Pat Schroeder (CO) asserted, "Regional Directors have weekly meetings to decide how to screw Democrats." As if the point had been lost on Jordan, Moore, and King, Lloyd Meeds (WA) told the men, "I blame the administration."

One of the foremost scholars of executive branch politics, Hugh Heclo (1983, 26–27), summed up the history of cabinet government this way: "It is significant that no president has ever left office extolling the virtues of cabinet government." He continues, telling us why:

---

[25] Quotes in this paragraph are taken from the handwritten notes of Tom Foley, *Congressional Papers of Thomas S. Foley*, Cage 655, House and Party Leadership Series, Box 194, Folder 12, "Minutes, June 14, 1977." These notes contain more frank language than is contained in the official minutes of this meeting of the Democratic Steering and Policy Committee.

First, the Constitution binds executive bureaucracies to a powerful legislature independent of the president. And, second, our constitutional system vests executive branch leadership in a president and department heads whose personal and political fates are not closely tied together.

The water wars were fought in an environment heavily influenced by the outsider Carter's initial belief in cabinet government. Successful cabinet government is difficult to achieve in most policy areas; in a policy area that is the text book example of subsystem politics, it is an even more daunting challenge. As Hamilton Jordan admitted to members of Congress, as early as June 1977, during a meeting with the House leadership, "Cabinet officers have already gone into business for themselves."[26]

CHANGES IN CONGRESS

Jimmy Carter's outsider campaign, transition, and governing style almost guaranteed that his presidency would encounter difficulties in congressional relations. Changes in Congress, some of which were enacted in response to the same pressures that helped elect Carter president (e.g., Watergate and Vietnam), further exacerbated the historic pull and tug of separation of powers, creating further challenges for Carter's legislative agenda.

When Jimmy Carter was inaugurated on January 20, 1977, it was the first time since 1969 and the Johnson administration that Congress and the White House were controlled by the same political party. As much as the country hoped to move beyond the twin memories of the Vietnam War and Watergate, Democrats

---

[26] Tom Foley, *Congressional Papers of Thomas S. Foley*, Cage 655, House and Party Leadership Series, Box 194, Folder 12, "Minutes, June 14, 1977."

(especially Jimmy Carter) hoped to instigate major policy changes. But Congress had changed in some significant ways during the previous eight years, seeking to reassert its institutional authority in the face of significant challenges from the executive branch. In the wake of Vietnam, Congress reasserted itself by passing the War Powers Act of 1973—over President Nixon's veto—which sought to limit presidential exercise of military power. Richard Nixon had argued that presidents had the inherent power of impoundment; the power to *refuse* to spend money appropriated by Congress. President Nixon's repeated refusal to spend money on social programs supported by congressional Democrats led to the passage of the Budget Impoundment and Control Act of 1974 in the final month of his presidency. Congress was reasserting its power of the purse. The Budget Impoundment and Control Act curtailed the use of impoundments by presidents.

Congress had also taken other important steps to reform its internal functions during this period. Decentralizing reforms were aimed at providing more opportunities for more members to influence the policy process. The Democratic Caucus passed rules that required that committee chairs be elected by the House Democratic membership rather than being guaranteed a leadership position based on their seniority. Theoretically, the election of chairs would make them more responsive to the desires of the full Democratic Caucus, which was becoming much more liberal. Indeed, three committee chairs were replaced during the first year of the new selection procedure. New rules, including the Subcommittee Bill of Rights, fragmented power by bolstering the power of congressional subcommittees and giving them a consistent voice in the policy process. Though less pronounced than in the House, similar decentralizing reforms were also taking place in the Senate; the natural decentralization of the Senate blunted the need for many of these reforms.

At the same time that Congress was decentralizing, it was also centralizing power in its leadership. The Speaker of the House was given important new powers over the committee assignment process, especially assignments of Democratic members to the Rules Committee, which exercises significant powers over the flow of legislation in the House. With a new focus on "party unity" (voting with the leadership on important votes), members of Congress were increasingly aware that many of their votes would be a function of "party policy," thereby influencing their future power in the House. The reforms in the budget process as a result of the Budget Impoundment and Control Act (BICA) were partially meant to centralize control over congressional budgeting. In addition to President Nixon's impoundment actions, BICA was aimed at dealing with consistent growth in budget deficits that were being blamed, in part, on Congress' inability to coordinate revenue and spending, ostensibly due to an unwillingness to control spending. Newly created Budget Committees in the House and Senate were intended to provide a blueprint for the revenue committees—Ways and Means in the House and Finance in the Senate—and its spending committees, House and Senate Appropriations. Deficit politics—the focus on balancing the nation's budget—had come to Washington.

This was a new Congress: more internally fragmented, more democratic, more liberal, and less reliant on seniority than in Johnson's day. Jimmy Carter's Congress was new in some other important ways. Almost a third of the membership of the House had been elected since the watershed election of 1974, when seventy-five new members, more aggressive, independent, and liberal, were elected to the House. The leadership in Jimmy Carter's Congress was also new; the Speaker, majority leader, and whip in the House, as well as the majority and minority leaders in the Senate, were all new to their positions when Jimmy Carter took the Oath of Office. A new president, new congressional leadership, and a new congressional membership added up to a very different strategic circumstance, well summarized by the head of President Carter's Office of Congressional Liaison, Frank Moore:

> A hundred and fifty new Democrats. Didn't come up through the party ranks; hadn't gone through all that discipline. Didn't owe anything to anybody...[Speaker] Tip O'Neill (D-MA) was new. Jim Wright (D-TX) was Majority Leader. He had been elected Majority Leader by one vote over Phil Burton (D-CA) after a bruising, bruising, three-way fight first...[Whip John] Brademas (D-IN), others who were brand new in their jobs. And not real sure of themselves in their jobs. With the Speaker looking out at 150 Democratic freshmen and sophomores who were fighting to overturn the seniority system, and demanding to elect their own chairmen, and doing it... deposing the Chairman of the Ag[riculture] Committee, and putting Tom Foley (D-WA) in, and opposing other chairmen. And you're supposed to be leading this group, and you look out that see all these people are overthrowing people you've served with for 30 years. You see them pushed off to the side; you become a little concerned about your own fate...[Then] you go to the Senate. And a new Majority Leader Robert C. Byrd [D-WV]...also in a contested race...he was brand new in his job.[27]

Despite potential sources of conflict between Carter and the Congress, early meetings between Carter and the congressional

---

[27] *Oral History Interview with Frank Moore*, Jimmy Carter Library and Museum, July 30–31, 2002, 59–60.

leadership initially evidenced a willingness of both sides to work together. Just three weeks after the election, Carter attended a luncheon at the Capitol with members of the leadership and struck a cooperative tone. In reference to Ford's frequent use of the veto, Carter told members of the leadership that "[t]he American people are ready for good relations between the White House and Congress...Pennsylvania Avenue is a two-way street...I want a substantive relationship with you."[28] Later, Carter reiterated his willingness to strike a different posture with Congress than did Ford: "With a Republican president you've had a difficult time, but with a Democratic president hopefully you won't find that difficulty."[29] But this initial meeting foreshadowed early difficulties between Carter and the leadership. Carter expressed three goals for his Administration: peace, economic recovery, and a balanced budget in four years. The then majority leader Tip O'Neill pledged his cooperation, but likely did not fully realize the president-elect's commitment to fiscal discipline above all other objectives. Carl Perkins' (D-KY) final comment at the meeting probably struck few as a future source of deep conflict when he warned the president not to be timid in his efforts to stimulate the economy: "[P]eople [don't] simply want temporary improvements but permanent ones such as water and other public works improvements."[30] At a second meeting about three weeks later at Blair House, differences

---

[28] Memorandum, "Speaker's Luncheon with President-Elect Carter," November 23, 1976, *John Brademas Congressional Papers*, Series 2, Box 4, folder 36, "Meetings with House Leadership."

[29] Ibid.

[30] Memorandum, "Speaker's Luncheon with President-Elect Carter," November 23, 1976, *John Brademas Congressional Papers*, Series 2, Box 4, folder 36, "Meetings with House Leadership."

on public works types of projects became more pronounced.[31] Recently elected majority leader Jim Wright raised the issue of public works projects with the president. Carter expressed his concern with relying on public works projects, arguing that they could only produce a small number of jobs, and expressed his interest in pursuing tax policy (either through a tax cut or tax rebate) to stimulate the economy. It may be easy, with the benefit of hindsight, to predict that the president and Congress were on a collision course only weeks before his inauguration, if not sooner, but this evidence from private meetings suggests that the early warning signs of impending conflict between the Democratic president and his congressional leaders were apparent.

---

[31] Memorandum, "Speaker's Luncheon with President-Elect Carter," November 23, 1976, *John Brademas Congressional Papers*, Series 2, Box 4, folder 36, "Meetings with House Leadership."

CHAPTER 3

WATER PROJECTS
AND THE EVOLUTION
OF THE VETO STRATEGY

Whether or not he wins the election and remains in Washington for another four years, Jimmy Carter will enter the books as a President who fought a running battle with Congress for nearly an entire term over how this country's water resources should be developed and paid for.
—Seth S. King, *New York Times*, October 1980

It is within the context described in chapter 2 that the water wars were waged. In the first year of the administration, Carter was cross-pressured between his fiscally conservative impulses, on the one hand, and his desire to develop a more cooperative relationship with Congress than Gerald Ford had experienced, on the other. In this chapter, we explore the initial salvos in the water wars, describing the evolution of the "veto strategy" in early 1978 as the administration found its moorings and the events that led to the veto fight. In chapter 4, we employ quantitative data to systematically assess efforts on both sides of the water wars.

THE WATER WARS: ROUND ONE 1977

A newly elected president has a short window at the beginning of his term to influence spending during the first fiscal year of his presidency. The budget for the president's first year is formulated the previous year by his predecessor; especially when the predecessor is of the opposite political party, the new president will want to influence the budget through supplemental appropriations. However, during his presidential transition, Carter's staff was not given the customary access to the internal reviews occurring at the Office of Management and Budget in the period between the election and the submission of the president's budget (Neustadt 1990, 241). Notes prepared by House Majority Whip John Brademas of a December 10, 1976, meeting between Carter and House leadership and staff report: "[Carter] said his people had been locked out of OMB, and that he knew nothing about the budget Ford will propose when he leaves office."[1] This limited access created difficulties in preparing a legislative agenda to send to Congress in one of the key areas that Carter planned to be active: reducing wasteful spending.

---

[1] Memorandum, "Speaker's Luncheon with President-Elect Carter," November 23, 1976, *John Brademas Congressional Papers*, Series 2, Box 4, folder 36, "Meetings with House Leadership."

Motivated by his interest in reducing the deficit by limiting pork barrel projects, Jimmy Carter created a list of nineteen projects that would be deleted, and instigated a review of 320 existing water projects with an eye toward trying to further reduce spending on projects that were deemed wasteful in economic terms, or that were considered environmentally unwise. Carter wrote to Congress:

> During the Campaign I committed myself to a prudent and responsible use of the taxpayers' money and to protection of the environment. Today I am announcing a major review of water projects, which will further both commitments…I have identified 19 projects which now appear unsupportable on economic, environmental, and/or safety grounds…I am recommending at this time that no funds be provided for these projects in FY 1978. I am instructing Secretary of the Interior Andrus, Secretary of the Army Alexander, working together with the Office of Management and Budget and the Council on Environmental Quality to carry out a complete evaluation of these 19 projects and of all other water resource projects and to develop comprehensive policy reforms in this critical area. They will report back to me and to the Congress by April 15. This review will give us the necessary facts upon which to make certain that only projects which are economically and environmentally sound will receive final approval. The FY 1978 budget reductions for the deleted projects about to $289 million. Total potential savings for these deleted projects would amount to $5.1 billion.[2]

The president had several concerns about water projects that drove his convictions. Cost-sharing with states was not considered

---

[2] "To the Congress of the United States," from the White House, Jimmy Carter Library, Office of the Congressional Liaison, Box 50, Water Projects 2/15/77–4/16/77.

in the appropriations process, leading the federal government to bear the lion's share of the cost of these projects. Furthermore, Carter sought to change the way that water projects were funded. Typically, water projects were funded one year at a time, which obscured the true total cost of the projects at full build out. Carter demanded full funding for the projects as a means of gaining control over the long-term costs of the projects and thereby causing Congress to be less of a spendthrift when it came to future projects.

The politically dangerous decision to target the water projects so soon after the hard feelings engendered by the election and transition has sometimes been attributed to overzealousness on the part of environmental activists on the White House staff. Domestic Policy Adviser Eizenstat refuted this assertion, claiming that the president was the driving force behind the decision:

> Well the President…asked for some alternatives in terms of saving money. And OMB has long had a view that water projects are not cost effective—at least a lot of them aren't—and I think that in some briefing paper they gave it to him. He fixed on it because he is and was a strong environmentalist, and viewed many of these things as boondoggles, the kind of waste that he had run against in the campaign, and as not environmentally sound in many instances, all of which was true. In the rush to have to get up this alternate budget, the so-called "hit-list" was prepared without time for consultation, without time to check, without time to discuss what the implications were. And far from being something the President was pushed to do by the staff, this was really his baby.[3]

---

[3] *Interview with Stuart Eizenstat*, January 29–30, Carter Presidency Project, Miller Center, 60. Elsewhere (Miller 1984, 287), Eizenstat referred to Carter as "the driving force from start to finish." The blame for the water projects decision is still frequently blamed on environmentally active staff, especially

Many of the projects on the hit list were in the districts of powerful members of the House, and in the states of powerful members of the Senate. According to a listing of the projects developed by the Office of Congressional Liaison, the affected House members included five committee chairs, fourteen sub-committee chairs, the majority leader, four members of the Ways and Means Committee, one member of Appropriations, and four of the nine Democrats on Rules. On the Senate side, projects slated for deletion affected the assistant majority leader, six committee chairs, three members of the Finance Committee, and three members of the Appropriations Committee.[4]

Less than a month after his inauguration, Jimmy Carter's honeymoon with Congress had come to an end; and congressional response was swift.[5] One of the projects on the hit list was in Louisiana. The Atchafalaya River Project affected the state of Louisiana senator Russell Long (D). Long, son of infamous Louisiana governor Huey P. Long, was one of the old bulls of the Senate. Elected in 1948, he had parlayed his electoral security into the position of Chairman of the powerful Senate Finance Committee. The bulk of the Carter legislative agenda—energy policy, economic stimulus, tax reform—fell within the

---

Kathy Fletcher, who worked for Eizenstat. Anne Wexler, who joined the White House staff as public liaison after the hit list controversy, told the authors, "I do think that the first water projects explosion was probably a mistake. That was the naivety of some of the people who worked for Stu" (Interview with the authors, August 2007, Washington, DC).

[4] Calculated by the authors from "Democrats Affected by Projects," Jimmy Carter Library, Office of Congressional Liaison, Box 50, Water Projects, 2/18/77–10/6/78.

[5] Not all of the congressional response was negative. Within Congress there was some sentiment in favor of the president's actions. On February 15, 1977, sixty-two House members and twelve Senators wrote to Carter supporting his efforts to reform water resources programs.

jurisdiction of Long's Senate Committee, and the suggestion that his water project might be in danger did not endear Carter and his aides to the senator. Following a February meeting with Long, Senate liaison Dan Tate reported to Frank Moore that Long had threatened to put the president's economic stimulus plan "in the deep freeze."[6] At that same meeting, Senator Muskie (D-ME), chair of the Senate Budget Committee, hinted that he might hold up consideration of the Budget Resolution to save his Dickey–Lincoln Project. "In short," Tate reported, "the president might not get what he wants unless certain members of Congress get what they want. The threat was hardly veiled."[7]

Conspicuous among the other projects that were targeted for review—though not targeted for immediate deletion—was the Tennessee–Tombigbee Waterway. This massive project sought to connect the Tennessee River at the extreme northeastern corner of Mississippi to the Tombigbee River in west-central Alabama. Proponents of the project argued that it was necessary to reduce the time and distance necessary to transport goods from the Ohio Valley and Tennessee Valley to the Gulf of Mexico (see Figure 1).[8] The project, authorized by the Public Works Committee in 1946, had two powerful champions in the

---

[6] It was at this meeting that Russell Long stood and introduced himself as the chairman of the Senate Finance Committee. This story was often cited as evidence that the White House staff was unaware of the names of key members of Congress. Russell Long told his biographer that he simply thought that those at the meeting would want to know who he was. Speaking of Carter's effort to target water projects, Long responded that it was "dumb, dumb, dumb, dumb" (Mann 1992, 342).

[7] Memo to Frank Moore from Dan Tate, Jimmy Carter Library, Office of Congressional Liaison, Box 50, Water Projects 2/18/77–10/6/78.

[8] For the definitive treatment of the Tennessee–Tombigbee Project, see Stine (1993). Frisch and Kelly (2006) discussed repeated attempts in the House to stop Tennessee–Tombigbee during the early 1980s.

FIGURE 1. The Tennessee–Tombigbee Waterway Project.

America's New Transportation Artery

Source. Senator John Stennis Papers, Mississippi State University.

Note. The Tennessee–Tombigbee Waterway Project sought to connect the Tennessee River to the Gulf of Mexico via a 263-mile waterway that would travel through Mississippi and Alabama. Proponents argued that it would be vital to the transportation of agricultural products and coal from several states (as indicated by shading).

House and Senate: Representative Tom Bevill (D-AL), chairman of the Energy and Water Subcommittee of Appropriations, and Senator John Stennis (D-MS), chairman of the analogous Public Works Subcommittee of Appropriations in the Senate. As the chairmen of the two subcommittees responsible for spending on water projects, they had a vested interest in protecting the bill into which they had inserted projects for their colleagues. As members of Congress from the two states most directly affected by Tennessee–Tombigbee, they had a vested interest in protecting their project. And part of protecting their project was protecting the projects of those who would vote on subsequent appropriations bills. Thus, even if Tennessee–Tombigbee was not on the hit list, these two men would have resisted Carter's maneuver; that they had a dog in the fight steeled their resistance.

The way in which many members of Congress found out about their endangered projects was as harmful to the White House as the proposed deletion of the projects themselves.[9] Rumors about possible additions to the hit list echoed in the silence left by the White House's miscommunication of the details of the list. Some members of Congress learned of the status of their projects in the newspaper rather than hearing from the president or the Office of Congressional Liaison. According to Moore, a great deal of "the problem was a lack of notification and consultation. I remember Bizz Johnson [D-CA] calling me. He said, 'I just got up and I've never been so upset in my whole life. I just read it in the paper.'"[10]

---

[9] Representative Mo Udall (D-AZ) referred to the release of the hit list as the "Washington's Birthday Massacre" (Reisner 1993, 315).

[10] *Interview with Frank Moore (including William Cable, Dan Tate, and Robert Thompson)*, Miller Center for Public Affairs Presidential Oral History Program, September 18–19, 1981, 119.

According to several accounts, the White House staff was in the process of notifying affected members of Congress when the media broke the story of the "hit list." Patricia (Pat) Bario of the White House Press Office claimed:

> The water project story came out while we were in the process of at least notification—if it wasn't consulting. I remember it well because it was a Saturday, and I was press duty officer, and suddenly we got all these irate phone calls about something we had not yet announced and I had not been briefed on. It was quite an interesting day.[11]

While they were angered about the way that they learned about the water projects decision, much of the outrage was targeted at the lack of prior consultation. Carter officials alternatively blame the lack of consultation on the exigencies of time in preparing the budget request, the belief that consultation would not be met well and give them a head's up, and so forth. Frank Moore was quoted by Martin Tolchin (1977, 1) of the *New York Times* as claiming, "Water projects were a deletion from the budget. I never knew it was the tradition to tell people what's going to be in the budget before it was being released."[12]

---

[11] *Interview with Jody Powell (including Claudia Townsend, Dale Leibach, Ray Jenkins, Rex Granum, Al Friendly, Patricia Bario)*, Miller Center for Public Affairs Presidential Oral History Program, December 17–18, 1981. Press Secretary Jody Powell contended that no amount of consultation would have assuaged congressional opposition to the decision to eliminate funding for the water projects. However, the failure to provide prior notification to many members allowed for Congress to use the issue as additional evidence of ineptitude in the Carter White House.

[12] On the broader question of the Carter administration and difficulties with consultation, see Moore et al., Oral History, 32–33. Moore blamed the fallout from Carter's early appointments, particularly two in Massachusetts that were made without first consulting Speaker O'Neill, as responsible for the

Regardless of the reason, the failure to consult with members of Congress before the hit list was made public gave opponents of the policy change the opportunity to equate the hit list with the growing sense of administration incompetence. Many members became suspicious regarding their own projects because of false lists that were circulating, which purported to contain a list of the threatened projects much larger than what the president proposed. As Frank Moore related it,

> [W]hat caused so much of the problem were the projects that were falsely listed. Some imaginary lists had dams on them that we had no intention of cutting, either because of completion or because they served some useful purpose—flood control, power generation or something. I guess every dam in the United States was on some of those lists that were floating around.[13]

Illustrating the hazards of Carter's initial reliance on cabinet government (described in chapter 2) on an issue where proposals were made to cut agency budgets, both the Interior Department and the Army Corps of Engineers were responsible for lists of projects that caused confusion and made the cuts appear to members of Congress to be even more severe that what was actually being proposed. In addition to the official list of nineteen projects proposed for deletion by the White House, there was a second list, supplied by the Army Corps of Engineers to Senator Stennis' subcommittee, which listed thirty-seven Corps

---

administration's reputation for failing to consult. This is consistent with our general discussion of how dissatisfied House members were with the pace of political appointments early in the administration (see chapter 2). See also Farrell (2001, esp. ch. 19).

[13] *Interview with Frank Moore (including William Cable, Dan Tate, and Robert Thompson)*, Miller Center for Public Affairs Presidential Oral History Program, September 18–19, 1981, 118.

projects that did not meet the criterion of a cost-benefit ratio of greater than one (benefits of the project exceeding the costs) when using the assumption of an interest rate of 6⅜%, and a third list of thirty-five projects targeted for additional review, prepared during the presidential transition, which was leaked by the Interior Department and confirmed by Secretary Andrus.[14]

Seeking further clarification, House and Senate members petitioned the White House for a meeting to discuss the projects that were targeted (and rumored to be targeted). Sixteen senators sent a telegram to the White House, stating, "These projects have an overwhelming economic and environmental impact on our states and we respectfully ask that we meet with you in the next few days to reflect our concerns."[15] Senate Majority Leader Robert Byrd informed the president by letter of the "strong feelings" of senators whose water projects were threatened: "The universal complaint—and I believe it is justified—is that these Senators were not consulted and given an opportunity for a discussion of the matter prior to the action taken."[16] Almost a month following the release of the hit list (March 10th), the White House held a briefing for House and Senate members affected by the new policy direction. Vice President Mondale, Director of OMB Bert Lance, and Secretaries Andrus and Alexander were scheduled to brief twenty-eight Senators and twenty-eight House members.

[14] Briefing for March 10, 1977, meeting, from Frank Moore and Stuart Eizenstat, March 9, 1977, Jimmy Carter Library, Office of Congressional Liaison Box. On the confusion caused by multiple lists, see Reisner (1993) and Miller (1984).

[15] Telegram to the White House, February 21, 1977, Jimmy Carter Library, Office of the Congressional Liaison, Box 50, Water Projects 2/15/77–4/16/77.

[16] Letter to the president from Robert Byrd, March 4, 1977, Jimmy Carter Library, Office of the Congressional Liaison, Box 50, Water Projects 2/15/77–4/16/77.

The president was not included on the initial agenda for the meeting; however, Carter was encouraged to appear at the meeting by Frank Moore, who had been hearing complaints from senators about lack of presidential involvement. Carter attended part of the meeting and expressed his sympathy with the legislators, citing his experiences as governor during the Spewrell Bluff Dam incident (see chapter 2), and assured them that he did not reach his decision lightly. Again stressing the economic and environmental imperatives, he assured members that the review of their projects would be open, and decisions would be made based on their merits, not politics.[17] The president reiterated his position in a letter to members several days later:

> I cannot meet my commitment to balance the budget unless the Congress and I can cooperate in reducing unnecessary spending. Every ongoing program in the government must be continually examined in the list of the harsh realities of a tight budget. I approached my decision to delete funding on certain water projects, to review all current projects, and to develop commitment to fiscal responsibility, environmental quality, and human safety.

His decisions, he stressed, were not arbitrary.[18] Reflecting on the meeting in his diary, Carter wrote: "Had a rough meeting with about thirty-five members of the Congress on water projects. They are raising Cain because we took those items out of their 1978 budget, but I am determined to push this item as much as

---

[17] Meeting with members of Congress on Water Resource Projects, Thursday March 10, 1977 (memo dated March 9, 1977), from Stu Eizenstat and Frank Moore, Jimmy Carter Library, Office of the Congressional Liaison, Box 50, Water Projects 2/15/77–4/16/77.
[18] Letter to members of Congress, March 16, 1977, Jimmy Carter Library, Office of the Congressional Liaison, Box 50, Water Projects 2/15/77–4/16/77.

possible" (Carter 1995, 82). In a private meeting on April 5 with the House and Senate Democratic leadership in the Family Dining Room at the White House, Senate Majority Leader Robert Byrd warned the president that his challenge of the water projects was endangering the rest of his legislative agenda:

> Mr. President, you raised the water projects question. Today in the Senate we would lose on the [tax] rebate. We'd get no more than 40 votes...I can't tell you, Mr. President, how much the water project list is doing to our efforts...Two senators from Mississippi are doubtful, and one of two in Alabama and Arizona. We've already lost two in Colorado and I think the Senator from Maine (Hathaway). If we were to have a vote today we would lose hands down. Some Senators aren't going to come along as long as those water projects are on the list. It's a battle you don't need. It will cost you—and us—here and on other, more important battles. Its timing was 100 percent off. Senator Long will vote for the rebate but he won't put his arm around any other Senator so long as water projects in his state are on the list. If we lose it would be a defeat for the President and for the Senate Democratic leadership. I want to be honest with you Mr. President. I'd be very insincere and dishonest with you if I didn't say this.[19]

Senator Hubert Humphrey (D-MN) concurred: "I agree with what Bob Byrd said on the tax rebate. We don't have a prayer of passing it at this time because of the water projects."[20]

Following a review of the targeted projects, the Carter administration recommended, on April 18, 1977, the deletion of nineteen water projects and significant changes in funding for five other projects. Consistent with his technocratic approach to the problem,

---

[19] "White House Leadership Meeting, Wednesday, April 5, 1977," 8–9, *Thomas P. O'Neill Papers*, Elizabeth Kelley Files, Box 9, Folder 3.
[20] Ibid.

Carter sought to convince the bicameral Democratic leadership of the rationality of his approach to the deletion of water projects:

> I feel very strongly about the need to show fiscal restraint. I hope that you can support our analysis on the water projects. We have gone back and assessed them in a very professional way with the Army Engineers and the Interior Department. I see developing an unnecessary confrontation with Congress.[21]

At no point in Carter's direct dealings with congressional leaders was the conflict between Carter's "new Democratic" philosophy and the New Deal/Great Society orientation of the leadership more apparent than in Tip O'Neill's response to Carter's plea for fiscal restraint. O'Neill responded at length:

> [Mr. President,] your programs are kind of unmindful that we have always been the champions of the poor and the indigent. There are 12 million people on welfare, 7 million of them children. And we have had a lot of programs to be helpful to them, and I see no desire in this Congress to cut back on programs that we have now or new programs. The basis of our party is liberal and you are going to have to appeal to them. If we are going to have cooperation and put your program through it must be a two-way street. We must have the Black Caucus, the support of metropolitan areas, for those who are dependent on us and on what government does. I can read this Congress, but if there is no move to serve those who need compassion we'll run into a heap of trouble.[22]

---

[21] "White House Leadership Meeting, Wednesday, May 3, 1977," 9–10, *Thomas P. O'Neill Papers*, Elizabeth Kelley Files, Box 9, Folder 3.
[22] Ibid., 6.

Carter retreated somewhat, responding that "perhaps we have excessively emphasized fiscal restraint. We don't want to appear callous and we are not wanting to rob the poor."[23] This exchange made clear the dramatic difference of perspective between the conservative Democrat and the more liberal leaders with whom he would need to work.

Regardless of the merits of Carter's case, his recommendations continued to meet with significant resistance from Congress; the water projects were another example of the difference of perspectives between Carter and the congressional leadership. At a leadership meeting at the White House on May 19, 1977, Jim Wright again warned the president of the potential damage that his stand on the water projects presented in the Congress; they engaged in the following exchange:

> WRIGHT: Mr. President, Fritz Hollings is getting out a newsletter that is getting a good deal of attention in the House, which lists the dollars going to foreign countries for water projects and notes that they are doing so without cost benefit justifications.
>
> CARTER: [*Smiling and blushing*] I was wondering how you would tie that in!
>
> WRIGHT: Mr. President, we're getting along fine despite the efforts of the news media. But I see this little cloud on the horizon no bigger than a man's hand...So before we get set in concrete on the water projects I'd like to bring in Tom Bevill, Bizz Johnson, and a half a dozen others to talk about it...Tom Bevill is trying, he's

---

[23] Ibid., 7.

modifying, eliminating, trying to be within your budget figures.

Carter: I am eager to get together.[24]

In an attempt to try to mend fences with at least one powerful member of the House, President Carter met privately eight days later with Chairman of the Public Works Subcommittee of the Appropriations Committee Tom Bevill. The Tennessee–Tombigbee Waterway Project was initially endangered by Carter's new water policy, but following the review, Carter had recommended continued funding for the project. Despite the reprieve for his own project, however, Bevill considered funding of water projects to be a congressional prerogative and insisted on funding for all projects, including those proposed for deletion by the president. At this meeting, Carter attempted to discuss why the projects were recommended for deletion, discussing each on a case-by-case basis, in an attempt to convince Bevill to support his position. Bevill left unconvinced. What the White House may not have understood was that Bevill's power as a subcommittee chair was being challenged; his ability to provide funding for other members' projects—and protect that funding—was the basis of his influence. To surrender on the other projects would undermine Bevill's power and could endanger the Tennessee–Tombigbee in the long term; without the support of other members, he would not be able to fend off future challenges to his project.

---

[24] "White House Leadership Meeting, Wednesday, May 19, 1977," 9–10, *Thomas P. O'Neill Papers*, Elizabeth Kelley Files, Box 9, Folder 3. "Smiling and blushing" is the description used to describe the president's reaction by John Brademas in his meeting notes.

With the congressional Democratic leadership and many powerful committee and subcommittee chairs lined up against him, Carter began assembling the votes necessary to sustain a veto. Special attention was focused on the more junior members of Congress. These junior members were familiar with the growing public discontent regarding budget deficits and did not have threatened projects in their districts—projects tended to be in the districts of more senior members who had the opportunity to build political support for their projects—thus they were likely to support Carter's efforts. Carter believed that he had the 146 votes necessary to sustain the veto if an override should be attempted (Carter 1995, 83). But an initial analysis at the time by the liaison's office in March 1977 indicated that the effort looked "pretty grim." According to Ann Dye's analysis, the president could probably count on 141 votes, and might be able to get a maximum 168 votes—either provided a slim margin on which to base a veto.[25]

On May 3, the House Energy and Water Subcommittee reported out their supplemental appropriations bill, including funding for all of the water projects that were targeted by the president. The president responded with a letter to Appropriations Committee members eight days later expressing concern and "disappointment" with their actions. Citing his commitment to balance the budget by 1981, Carter warned that "if wasteful spending is to be curtailed…and the Budget balanced by FY 1981, the Congress will have to assist me in eliminating needless and counterproductive projects."[26] Meeting with House

---

[25] Memo to Frank Moore from Ann Dye, March 14, 1977, Jimmy Carter Library, Office of Congressional Liaison, Box 50, Water Projects 2/18/77–10/6/78.

[26] Letter from Jimmy Carter to Congressman Joe Addabbo, May 11, 1977, Jimmy Carter Library, White House Central File, Box FG-150, Folder FG-53-2 1/20/77–1/20/81.

Figure 2. Jimmy Carter and Tom Bevill meet for a private lunch in the Oval Office.

Source. Courtesy of the Jimmy Carter Library and Museum.
Note. Jimmy Carter and Tom Bevill (D-AL) met for a private lunch in the Oval Office. Carter sought to convince the subcommittee chair to support the deletion of eighteen water projects from his subcommittee's appropriations bill. Bevill left unconvinced.

proponents of water projects—Majority Leader and Public Works Committee member Jim Wright; Chairman of the Public Works Committee Bizz Johnson (D-CA); Gunn McKay (D-UT), a member of the Appropriations Committee; Tom Bevill; and Jamie Whitten (D-MS), the ranking Democrat on the Appropriations Committee—Carter reiterated his position on the projects. Mentioning the possibility of a veto, the men sought—but did not find—a solution to the impasse.

Full committee consideration of the subcommittee bill endorsed the subcommittee's action, and the first floor battle was set. The House standard-bearer for the president's position was Butler Derrick (D-SC), who, along with Silvio Conte (R-MA), a long-time opponent of pork barrel spending, offered an amendment representing the administration's position to strip all eighteen of the water projects from the Appropriations Committee Bill. On June 13, 1977, the "Derrick Amendment" was defeated on the House floor by a surprisingly small margin, 194–218; funding for all of the projects remained in the Energy and Water Appropriations Bill for the time being.

An analysis of the vote performed by the liaison's office several days later indicated the tactical situation following the House votes. The House was split along regional lines with members from the Northeast and the Midwest supporting the president's position 137–52, and members from the South and West opposed to the president's position 44–145. The Appropriations Committee and Public Works Committee were significant sources of opposition to the president (15–39 and 7–37 in opposition to the president's position, respectively), while the Watergate Babies of 1974 were generally with the president 57–29. Support for Carter's position in the House would need to be cobbled together through reliance on a regional coalition of the northeast–midwest members, the Class of 1974, at least sixty Republicans, and members of the Budget Committee, among others.[27]

Derrick's support of the administration's position might be considered surprising. Included in the hit list was the Richard B. Russell's lake project, which spanned Georgia and South Carolina, and was partially located in his district: $21 million of funding was at stake. Traditional theories of congressional

---

[27] Memorandum for Frank Moore from Rick Merrill, "Water Projects Vote in the House," Jimmy Carter Library. Office of Congressional Liaison, Box 50, Water Projects 2/18/77–10/6/78.

behavior stress the reelection motivation, that is, they suggest that given members' overwhelming desire to be reelected, they will support spending that benefits their district—often over the national interest—to reap the rewards of a grateful electorate. Butler Derrick, then, seems an anomaly. Elected as one of the Watergate Babies in the 1974 Democratic congressional land-slide, Derrick was a reformer sympathetic with the deficit control philosophy that Carter brought to the White House. And when push came to shove, Derrick chose principle over his concern about reelection.

The following week, the battle moved to the Senate Appro-priations Committee Subcommittee on Public Works, chaired by John Stennis. Perhaps surprised by the close vote on the Derrick Amendment, the subcommittee recommended no funding for nine of the nineteen projects targeted by the president, and half funding for the Bayou Bodcau Project in Louisiana, the home state of Finance Committee Chair Russell Long and Energy and Natural Resources Committee member Bennett Johnston (D-LA). It included full funding for the Richard B. Russell Dam Project in Georgia and South Carolina. The subcommittee action also included some modifications of five other projects that were suggested by the president. However, the Central Utah Project was a source of concern that Domestic Policy Adviser Stuart (Stu) Eizenstat indicated in a memo to the president: "The Subcommittee fully funded the unmodified project...you have privately indicated to Frank [Moore] and me that you have an objection to this funding."[28] Reacting to the Senate action, key House allies on water issues—Butler Derrick, George Miller

---

[28] Memorandum for the president from Stu Eizenstat, June 20, 1977, Jimmy Carter Library, Office of Congressional Liaison, Box 50, Water Projects 2/18/77–10/6/78.

(D-CA), Tom Downey (D-NY), Abner Mikva (D-IL), and Phil Burton (CA)—informed House Liaison Jim Free of their advice to the president to "hang tough on the water projects...[they say] he should not compromise."[29]

Stennis' subcommittee had delivered half of a victory to the president, but the question remained, as the bill went to conference, whether the president should support the Stennis compromise or push for his whole list of deletions. One of the chief considerations was the inclusion of the Russell Project. As Eizenstat pointed out in a memo to the president: "Our amendment's prime sponsor in the House, Butler Derrick, opposed the project at great personal risk"—the implication being that shifting position would harm an important House ally. Eizenstat also considered the long-term implications of a compromise. He felt that the president should "at least make an effort to knock out all of the projects in the Senate (and then support Senator Stennis' position or some similar compromise as a fallback position). To do otherwise may put us in a weak position in the conference." Eizenstat warned the president of the implications of a compromise:

> "[I]n order to get congressional passage of our water reform policy in the near future and in the long term, we will need the full support of those congressmen who voted with us to knock out all of the projects. Therefore, at this stage, we should take no action which signals to them a retreat from the Administration's determination."[30]

---

[29] Note from Jim Free to Frank Moore, June 23, 1977, Jimmy Carter Library, Office of Congressional Liaison, Box 50, Water Projects 2/18/77–10/6/78.

[30] Memorandum for the president from Stu Eizenstat, June 20, 1977, Jimmy Carter Library, Office of Congressional Liaison, Box 50, Water Projects 2/18/77–10/6/78.

Taking Eizenstat's advice, the administration backed a Senate floor amendment offered by New Hampshire Democrat Thomas McIntyre to strip the projects recommended by the president. Like the Derrick Amendment in the House, the McIntyre Amendment also failed.

With the Stennis compromise intact in the Senate version of the bill, as well as full funding in the House Bill, Energy and Water Appropriations legislation moved into conference. Carter was in a reasonably strong position should he choose to veto the legislation. The Derrick Amendment had come close to passing, and many of those votes could be counted on to sustain the president's veto if he chose to exercise it; the 198 votes exceeded earlier estimates of around 140 to 160 votes to sustain a veto. Speaker Tip O'Neill was anxious to avoid a veto battle; such a battle could obstruct the Democratic policy agenda that was working its way through Congress:

> "If the Congress were to override [an appropriations bill] the damage to Carter would be considerable. This argues strongly for an accommodation. Even an override attempt that failed would be damaging as we go forward with energy, tax reform, health insurance, reorganization, and other critical legislation."[31]

Pressured on one side by the congressional leadership and a congressional insurgency, and by his desire to promote the interests of a first-year Democratic president on the other, O'Neill brokered a deal between the party leadership and the leadership of the Appropriations Committee in Congress. He presented it to President Carter in a phone call to the White House. Based on

---

[31] Memorandum to the Speaker from Irv Sprague, June 1, 1977, "Vetoes," Jimmy Carter Library, Office of Congressional Liaison, Box 112, Speaker Memos. See also Farrell (2001, 460–462).

the Stennis compromise reached in the Senate, Congress agreed to delete some of the water projects and remove the Clinch River Breeder Reactor that Carter opposed from the bill; in return, the president would sign the appropriations bill.

President Carter's final action was a call to Butler Derrick to inform him that he had accepted the compromise. As Derrick recalled:

> My assistant said "the President is on the line." The President said, "I will not be vetoing the water bill." I replied "Mr. President, I have told members of the House that you would veto. Many, especially the new members have gone against the 'Old Bulls.' You are correct on the issue. You will lose credibility in the Congress." He did not veto. He never fully regained his credibility in the House.

According to Derrick, the decision not to veto was a critical moment in the Carter presidency. "I do believe the 'water bill' was, to a large degree, the downfall of his administration. Not because he was not on the correct side of the issue, he was, but when he 'blinked' he wrote the obituary for his administration and a second term."[32]

ROUND ONE: DECISION AND FALLOUT

As far back as the pre-inauguration transition meetings with the congressional leadership, Carter and the congressional leadership had stressed accommodation and avoidance of "policy vetoes." Carter was receiving advice from some of his staff to not veto. As Les Francis described, "[W]hen the first water projects bill came through we weighed in—those of us who primarily were in congressional relations and the political side and others—on

---

[32] Telephone interview with the authors, April 2008.

the side of not vetoing."[33] Without consulting with his aides, Carter accepted O'Neill's compromise on the spot. Considering the terms of the agreement, Carter accepted the deal, concluding that he had made significant progress on a set of issues of great importance to him. But Domestic Policy Adviser Stu Eizenstat, who was in the Oval Office at the time of the phone call, told the president that his action undermined the positions of his most staunch congressional allies. Eizenstat's primary objection to compromise was that Carter had not conferred with his allies on the Hill who would likely feel betrayed.

> I was in the study when the call came in from Tip O'Neill. Tip told the president that we needed to show a face of unity, that we needed to avoid a veto. He proposed a deal whereby they would split the difference—half would be funded and half would not be funded, fifty/fifty. And the president agreed. He made the decision, without Frank Moore, without staff consultation. And I said to him, you can't do that, we have 194 Democrats who will support you, what did you do? We lost both ways.[34]

House Liaison Jim Free described his reaction to the compromise:

> Well I raised a lot of hell with my colleagues in the White House. We were in the process of putting together a coalition that would have maybe 200+ members that the leadership in the House would realize that we could get support for our initiatives without them and they

---

[33] Interview with the authors, August 2007, Washington, DC.

[34] Remarks at the Carter Conference, January 2007, Athens, Georgia. See also Eizenstat Oral History, 61. The decision to make the deal has erroneously been attributed to Hamilton Jordan (see Reisner 1993, 320). While Jordan may have recommended that the president accept a deal, he was not present when the conversation occurred.

would follow us…we could lead. I caught hell from the members who had pledged to support us. Silvio Conte was furious…The hardest conversation was with Butler Derrick who felt betrayed.[35]

Complicating the relationship with Derrick was the fact that Jim Free had used Derrick's office as his home base for his lobbying efforts (and he later married one of Butler Derrick's staff members). Furthermore, Free noted that

…in the end the deal was about the authorization of Clinch River, and Clinch River hadn't been authorized! I could have told them that if they had asked me. And you know Jim Wright and the others on Public Works were just laughing when they heard about *that* deal."[36]

Likewise, Les Francis viewed the compromise as a mistake in the long run: "It sent a signal—inadvertently I think—it sent a signal or was received as a signal by people on the Hill that they could roll us."[37]

True to Eizenstat's prediction, Carter's congressional allies did feel betrayed by the president's reversal, and the decision to forgo a veto emboldened members of Congress who concluded that the president could be convinced to accept legislation on Congress' terms.[38] According to Frank Moore, the administration paid a price for its hesitation to cast a veto. Up to that point,

the President had stuck with them all [the projects] and then the Speaker called up one afternoon and sort of

---

[35] Interview with Jim Free, August 2007, Washington, DC.
[36] Ibid.; emphasis original.
[37] Ibid.
[38] In an anonymous telephone interview with the authors (August 2006), one of Carter's allies expressed the sense of betrayal but chose to blame Frank Moore for the reversal rather than the president, whom the interviewee described as a friend.

offered some kind of an accommodation…And some people felt of Carter 'he won't stand up, they won't stand up for what they believe; you can roll them if you work hard enough at it.' They interpreted it as a sign of weakness.[39]

Failure to veto the appropriations for these water projects in 1977 was judged by Carter, in retrospect, as a miscalculation:

This compromise bill should have been vetoed because, despite some attractive features, it still included wasteful items which my congressional supporters and I had opposed. Signing this act was certainly not the worst mistake I ever made, but it was accurately interpreted as a sign of weakness on my part, and I regretted it as much as any budget decision I made as president. (Carter 1995, 84)

In a signing statement[40] attached to the FY 1978 Energy and Water Supplemental Appropriations Bill, President Carter expressed his conviction to continue to pursue continued fiscal economy and policy changes in the FY 1979 Energy and Water Appropriations Bill. Carter pledged further action on the ten projects that continued under the compromise, de-authorization of the projects that were not funded in the supplemental appropriations bill, and additional reforms that met his policy goals, such as full funding of water projects, users fees, and local cost sharing arrangements. In the face of a compromise that Carter disliked, he had two major courses of action that he could pursue during FY 1978. First, he could have deferred spending on

---

[39] *Oral History Interview with Frank Moore*, Jimmy Carter Library and Museum, July 30–31, 2002, 109.

[40] This is a formal statement of the president, given when he affixes his signature to legislation. This usually indicates some future action or understanding of the legislation.

the funded projects; a deferral, however, could be overturned by either chamber of Congress and probably would have been. Second, he could rescind spending, that is, make a recommendation to cut the spending; in the absence of action by both chambers, the rescission would remove the money from the federal budget. Eizenstat and Moore, along with others, recommended against deferral or rescission, arguing that they would not succeed, and they would turn an apparent victory (Carter had gotten about half of what he wanted in terms of spending) into a defeat when Congress acted to stop the rescission. Furthermore, a rescission might endanger other priority legislation that would be coming before Congress.[41] Instead, Eizenstat and company counseled Carter to attach a deferral to his FY 1979 budget request, which would put off another confrontation until the beginning of the next year and legally defer spending until congressional action on the FY 1979 budget. It was this recommendation that Jimmy Carter endorsed by simply writing "ok—J" at the bottom of the memo.

The decision not to veto in 1977 took its toll on Carter's reputation on the Hill. It undermined the trust of Carter's congressional allies, making subsequent vetoes more difficult to defend in Congress. Once bitten and twice shy, members were less likely to trust Carter's congressional liaison staff and required assurances from those higher up:

> [I]t was a lot harder the next time, when the president did
> veto the appropriations bill. It took a lot of phone calls
> from people higher up than me. It took calls from the

---

[41] Memorandum to the president from Stu Eizenstat, Frank Moore, Bo Cutter, Secretary of the Army Clifford Alexander, and Assistant Secretary of the Interior Guy Martin, "Follow-up Strategy on Water Projects," September 8, 1977, Jimmy Carter Library, Office of Congressional Liaison, Box 50, Water Projects 2/18/77–10/6/78.

president. I think that if the president would have vetoed the first bill things would have be very different, but we will never know. We would have been able to show congressional leadership that we could get the votes for our initiatives.[42]

Failure to follow through on the veto threat increased the cost of future vetoes by ensuring that more resources (the time and effort of those higher up in the administration) would be necessary for sustaining a veto. It reinforced the growing suspicion on the Hill that Carter could be taken advantage of, could be "rolled," by Congress, and that Carter lacked core convictions. According to Free, it demonstrated "[n]ot only that we could be rolled, but that we didn't really believe in what we said we believe in; that there were no core beliefs that we would fight for."[43]

ROUND TWO: THE VETO STRATEGY

By the end of his first year in office, Carter's presidency was subject to serious criticism by members of Congress (the 1977 appropriations fight was a major source of this criticism, as was the battle over the Panama Canal Treaty), the media, and the public. His early decision to favor fiscal control over fiscal stimulus, which partially played out in the water projects fight, caused Carter to seem indecisive and feckless. There were other criticisms: that the administration was trying to do too much, that Carter's style in scaling down the perquisites of the presidency were shrinking the office in the public mind,[44] that Carter had too

---

[42] Interview with Jim Free, August 2007, Washington, DC.

[43] Ibid.

[44] For instance, White House breakfast meetings with the congressional leadership consisted of coffee and Danish pastries, much to the dismay of members who attended these breakfast meetings. Such spartan offerings became so

many Georgians in the White House and not enough staff with Washington experience, that Carter was too deeply involved in the "details" of governing, and that he was not tough enough with the Soviets.[45] According to Carter's advisers, it was necessary for him to forcefully present the "basic theme for your presidency—*the willingness to take on the tough problems, to make the difficult decisions.*"[46]

Transforming the president's public image, and his image in Congress, became a priority during the second year of Carter's presidency. In his dealings with Congress, a focus on developing a "veto strategy" took center stage. During the first year of his presidency, Carter was reluctant to use the veto. According to Hubert L. "Herky" Harris of OMB, there was an implicit " 'no veto' policy in the first year, an incredible decision on our part. We took away the one weapon of the presidency... When we would try to get something vetoed, someone said, 'we can't veto that, we'll look like Ford.' "[47] According to OMB Director Jim McIntyre, Carter's orientation toward the veto developed in part because

---

emblematic of the Carter White House style that when Ronald Reagan began having meetings with the congressional leadership and continued the practice of offering rolls and coffee, Senator Paul Laxalt (R-NV) complained to Max Friersdorf, "Rolls and coffee just don't do it... Let's not be cheap like Carter." Despite the complaint, Friersdorf recommended continuing the rolls and coffee regimen. Ronald Reagan Library, Kenneth Duberstein Files, Series I, Box 1 "Friersdorf Memos February 1981," Memo from Friersdorf to Jim Baker, Ed Meese, and Mike Deaver "Republican Congressional Leadership Meeting," February 24, 1981.

[45] Memorandum to the president, no author, "Projecting an Image," Jimmy Carter Library, Personal Secretary Handwriting File, Box 65, Folder 12/27/77.

[46] Ibid.; emphasis in original.

[47] *Interview with James McIntyre*, Miller Center of Public Affairs Presidential Oral History Program, October 28–29, 1981, 25.

[h]e had made a personal commitment to try to get along with the Congress, particularly since it was a Democratically controlled Congress. That was part of the explanation for his unwillingness to use the veto the first two years of the administration."[48]

In addition, the experience of the Nixon-Ford era shaped the decision on vetoes:

"[W]e should have started [vetoing] early, but there was so much of a psychological overhang from the way Nixon and Ford had had to govern by vetoing bills and then trying to sustain it that…we just said, President Carter said, he's just going to sign a bill, he's going to sign it."[49]

In fact, in an early meeting with the House Democratic leadership, Speaker Tip O'Neill stated his position that there should be "no policy vetoes." O'Neill forcefully argued that

if the Administration wanted to differ with Congress on details, that was alright, but with respect to policy matters, agreement should be worked out beforehand, and we should not let ourselves get into a situation where the president is vetoing bills involving matters of policy, and where there is a party position.[50]

In April 1978, McIntyre sent a memo to the president outlining the then-current veto policy: "[W]e seem now to consider vetoes

---

[48] *Interview with James McIntyre*, Miller Center of Public Affairs Presidential Oral History Program, October 28–29, 1981, 25–26.

[49] *Oral History Interview with Frank Moore*, Jimmy Carter Library and Museum, July 30–31, 2002, 99.

[50] Memorandum, "Speaker's Luncheon with President-Elect Carter at Blair House," December 10, 1976, *John Brademas Congressional Papers*, Series 2, Box 4, folder 36, "Meetings with House Leadership."

as <u>major</u> exercises of presidential power: Presidential actions which signify extraordinarily significant differences between Congress and the Administration and which, therefore, are almost inappropriate actions by a Democratic President with a Democratic Congress." As a result, he continued, "The Hill perceives our extreme reluctance to use the veto, and predictably, is less willing to negotiate over a wide range of issues." McIntyre counseled a new approach:

> I think we should modify our approach to the veto. It should not be considered a fundamental breakdown in relationships...I believe that if we were more ready to indicate disagreement by veto...we would create a greater respect and concern for our position on the Hill, and provide a stimulus for greater agency support of your positions[51]

McIntyre noted that FDR held the record for vetoing an average of fifty bills per year; Carter responded in the margin noting, "I averaged 70/yr as governor." By surrendering the veto, the president had surrendered "the one thing a president can control in the legislative calendar to an extent—the veto. You can determine when to veto it and send it back."[52] This view is consistent with Richard Neustadt's famous characterization of the veto as "a means of enforcing congressional and agency respect for presidential preferences or programs" (Neustadt 1954, 656).

---

[51] Memorandum for the president from Jim McIntyre, April 5, 1978, Jimmy Carter Library, Personal Secretary Handwriting File, Box 79, Congressional Veto Policy 4/10/78; emphasis (underline) in original.
[52] *Interview with Frank Moore (including William Cable, Dan Tate, and Robert Thompson)*, Miller Center for Public Affairs Presidential Oral History Program, September 18–19, 1981, 112.

Director of the Office of Congressional Liaison Frank Moore and Special Assistant to the President Les Francis summarized their feelings about the strategic position of the president in mid-1978:

> Both in the halls of Congress and among the public at large, runs a quietly spoken but nonetheless danger-ous theme: that Jimmy Carter isn't tough enough to be President, that he is inconsistent, that he doesn't have a grasp on the Presidency…We believe, as do others within the Administration, that this feeling is at the root of our continuing problems with Congress. Quite frankly, we believe our biggest problem with Congress—one which has a tremendous "spin-off" effect with the public—is that we are not taken seriously, that you simply do not enjoy the level of respect to which you are legitimately entitled.[53]

Stu Eizenstat, head of the Domestic Policy Council, came to a similar conclusion, writing to President Carter: "I am convinced that your rating in the public opinion polls is increasingly a func-tion of your relations with Congress and their capacity to pass legislation."[54] By choosing to veto an appropriations bill, Moore and Francis believed that the administration could achieve three interrelated goals:

> We can force a lid on spending, thus holding the deficit down and relieving inflationary pressures…we can dem-onstrate to the Congress that you can—and will—play hardball politics if you have to…we can show the public

[53] Memorandum to the president from Frank Moore and Les Francis, "Strategy on Various Appropriations Bills and Other Troublesome Legislation," June 5, 1978, Jimmy Carter Library, Office of Congressional Liaison, Box 26, Con-gressional Veto Policy 7/29/77–10/10/79.

[54] Memorandum to the President from Stu Eizenstat, February 21, 1978, Jimmy Carter Library, Personal Secretary Handwriting File, Box 23, 2/21/78.

that you are strong and very much in charge of the government.[55]

The decision to use the veto required a well-thought-out strategy that would require possible floor fights to sustain a veto, possibly in both chambers. In addition, Moore and Francis argued,

> We need to put interest groups on notice that they have been too greedy, and that we're ready to go after their pet programs. And we need to prepare the public for the coming confrontation. In short, if we are going to have a fight with Congress, let's do it right.[56]

That the president would use his veto was established. That he would use it on an appropriations bill was likely, given Moore and Francis' argument. That he would use it to veto the Energy and Water Appropriations Bill became apparent as the legislation developed within Congress. That his veto would be sustained was far from certain—this would require a major effort on the part of the White House and the president himself, as well as shape the relationship between Congress and the president for the remainder of his term.

Between February 6, 1978, and April 13, 1978, the House Appropriations Subcommittee on Public Works held hearings on the proposed appropriations bill. During these hearings, administration officials from the various agencies funded by the bill justified appropriations requests, reported on administration policy, and responded to queries about ongoing projects and

---

[55] Memorandum to the president from Frank Moore and Les Francis, "Strategy on Various Appropriations Bills and Other Troublesome Legislation, June 5, 1978, Jimmy Carter Library, Office of Congressional Liaison, Box 26, Congressional Veto Policy 7/29/77–10/10/79; emphasis (underline) in original.
[56] Ibid.

agency priorities. During the hearings, members of Congress often testified before the subcommittee to air their requests for project funding (though some did not, preferring the less public approach of requesting funding via letters and discussions with the subcommittee chair and his staff). On May 3, 1978, the subcommittee considered the "chairman's mark," that is, Tom Bevill's proposed appropriations bill. At this point in the process, a bill is typically refined but rarely ever changed in a significant fashion; H.R. 12928, however, was on its way.

Included in the chairman's mark were a number of provisions that would draw the attention of the administration. First and foremost was funding for the nine projects that were suspended as a result of the compromise surrounding the FY 1978 Public Works Appropriations Bill. It was unclear whether the compromise that Carter and Speaker O'Neill had agreed to the year before was binding for only FY 1978, or whether the projects were to be cancelled permanently. Whatever the case, Bevill did not feel bound by the 1977 deal and inserted funding for these projects into his bill. In addition, Bevill included new project starts for forty-six projects, compared to the twenty-six recommended by the administration, along with ten new planning starts. According to the White House, the forty-six projects had an estimated cost of $1.4 billion, which was considerably more than the administration's budget, which funded twenty-six projects with a cost of $700 million. Carter also objected to $100 million in accelerated funding for existing projects. Conspicuously left out of Bevill's bill was the president's proposal to consider new water projects under an assumption of "full funding," that is, appropriating the total cost of water projects. Full funding was a major Carter priority.[57]

---

[57] Letter from the president to members of Congress, June 12, 1978. Jimmy Carter Library, Personal Secretary Handwriting File, 6/12/78.

Taking advantage of the subcommittee passage of his bill, Tom Bevill's office announced via a press release that [f]unds totaling $192.7 million were recommended for major water resource systems in Alabama," and that his marquee project, the Tennessee–Tombigbee, was slated to receive $156 million of that total, an amount that represented "the maximum construction capability of the Corp of Engineers."

Bevill acknowledged that the bill included many projects not recommended by the administration, but stated that "the projects in question are economically justified and need to be continued." He continued, "Opponents of water projects seem to be centering their efforts around delaying work on certain projects...obviously if you delay construction long enough, inflation will eventually catch up to the point where costs will outweigh benefits."[58]

According to the release, Bevill expected full committee consideration on May 31, 1978. On the day of full committee consideration, OMB Director Jim McIntyre wrote to the chairman of the Appropriations Committee, George Mahon, warning that the Bevill bill contained elements that were unacceptable to the administration, including "significant funding increases" and failure to include a full funding provision. Seeking to diplomatically indicate the president's position on the bill, McIntyre reminded Chairman Mahon, "The President has indicated a special interest in this bill, and will be monitoring congressional activity closely." The subcommittee's bill was considered by the full Appropriations Committee at a mark-up session on May 31 and reported to the full House on June 1, 1978, without the

---

[58] Press release from the Office of Congressman Tom Bevill, May 3, 1978, *Tom Bevill Congressional Papers*, Box 6542, Folder 5.

significant changes indicated in McIntyre's letter.[59] A week later, on June 8, 1979, the Rules Committee granted a rule for the bill, and the rule and the legislation were ready for floor consideration. A day earlier, warning bells were sounding in OMB about the Public Works Appropriations Bill; Herky Harris alerted Frank Moore that the House was ready to begin floor proceedings on the bill, which included "significant discretionary increases above the amounts recommended in the President's budget and also contain[s] other objectionable provisions."[60] Three days before House action on the bill, House Liaison Jim Free joined the president in a meeting with thirty members of Congress at the White House. Following the meeting, Free indicated that "Members of Congress think this is the worst White House in fifty years...it was a very rough meeting." But Free fully understood why: "We are changing the rules on pork barrel politics." He concluded by referring to one of the president's chief goals: "[F]ull funding is going to be tough."[61]

June 15 and 16 brought the first tests of Chairman Bevill's bill on the House floor. The Carter administration was not without friends in the House, and their allies had agreed to offer a series of amendments aimed at modifying the bill to be consistent with the president's position. Carter advised members of Congress to support a series of amendments that would be offered to move

---

[59] Letter to the Honorable George Mahon from James McIntyre, Jr., May 31, 1978, Jimmy Carter Library, Office of Congressional Liaison, Box 155, Appropriations 6/8/77–7/7/78.

[60] Memorandum to Frank Moore from Hubert Harris, "House Floor Action on Appropriations Bills for Next Week," June 7, 1978, Jimmy Carter Library, Office of Congressional Liaison, Box 155, Appropriations 6/8/77–7/7/78.

[61] Memo from Steve Selig, "Congressional Liaison Meeting—6/13/78," Jimmy Carter Library, Chief of Staff (Selig), Box 171, Congressional Liaison 2/10/78–7/3/78.

the bill closer to his position: the Edgar Amendment, which would strip out the eight disputed projects that Bevill had included in his bill; the Miller Amendment, which would replace the forty-six projects proposed by Bevill with the twenty-six recommended by the president; and the Derrick Amendment, which would provide for full funding. Carter concluded his letter to Congress by warning: "Budgetary constraints and inflation make it imperative that the appropriations process be responsible and restrained. Sound projects and programs should be funded at reasonable rather than excessive levels. I cannot approve the proposed legislation in its present form."[62] The final sentence was pregnant with political meaning: the president was warning Congress of his willingness to veto the legislation.

The votes on the Edgar Amendment, in particular, would be an important test of the ability of the president to assemble a coalition capable of sustaining his promised veto. As it turned out, the vote on the Edgar Amendment to strip funding for eight objectionable projects was a lopsided defeat for the administration, with 142 votes supporting Edgar and the administration, and 234 supporting Bevill's bill. Bevill could only see this as a major victory; he needed less than sixty votes to override the promised veto.

On September 20, 1978, a group of forty-five senators wrote to Carter indicating that the bill would be on his desk shortly, and suggesting that he sign the legislation. The bipartisan letter gave a strong indication that if the president vetoed the bill, his veto would be overridden. The senators warned, "[W]e urge you to give your careful attention and your every consideration

---

[62] Letter from the president to members of Congress, June 12, 1978, Jimmy Carter Library, Personal Secretary Handwriting File, 6/12/78.

to the strong and overwhelming congressional support of this highly important measure before acting on any [veto] recommendations" from administration officials. As the senators pointed out, the Senate version of the bill had passed by a vote of 89–5, a seemingly veto-proof majority. Needing thirty-four votes in the Senate to sustain the veto, the signatures of forty-five senators—forty-five guaranteed "yes" votes—indicated that with only twenty-two more, the votes in the Senate would override the president's veto. The signal from the Senate was clear: sign the bill or expect to be overridden.[63]

Adding his voice to the chorus of congressional advice, Majority Leader Jim Wright sent an awkwardly typed "personal note" to the president on September 26, 1978 ("I'm typing it myself," the majority leader wrote). In the letter, Wright warned the president that the planned veto of the appropriations bill could interfere with his energy bill, which was pending congressional action. In language that could be interpreted as either a warning (from a Democratic leader) or a threat (from a member seeking the benefits that the Public Works appropriation contained), Wright told the president:

> The point of this message is that what you do on the water bill could have a serious—perhaps even decisive—effect upon our chances to adopt the Energy package. A veto of Public Works would, in my opinion, place the energy bill inconsiderably greater jeopardy than it is at the moment.

Wright warned that a veto would engender bitterness in the House. He concluded, "It is a question of relative national priorities, and the decision must be yours. Knowing your personal

---

[63] Letter to the president signed by forty-five Senators, September 20, 1978, *Tom Bevill Congressional Papers*, Box 6542, Folder 7.

predilections on the water subject, I expect it is a hard one for you. In my view, it's a fight none of us need [Wright had crossed out "none of us need" and wrote by hand "you don't need"], and one which the nation itself can ill afford at this time."[64] Carter read the letter carefully, underlining several of the pivotal passages. While it is impossible to know with certainty whether the president perceived it as a threat or as friendly advice, given the tension surrounding the impending veto, it was probably interpreted as a threat to derail the energy bill.

Shortly after Wright's letter, Wright, along with Tom Bevill and Senator Bennett Johnston, approached the White House with a possible compromise that would avert a veto *fight*, but not a veto. Carter's closest advisers on the issue were willing to consider a compromise, but, given their perceived strong bargaining position, they felt that any compromise should not stray substantially from the president's established position. Furthermore, wanting to avoid the mistakes and hard feelings caused by the compromise on water projects the previous year, they cautioned that the president would have to consult with his key House allies, such as "Butler Derrick, Bob Edgar, Dick Bolling (D-MO), and Ab Mikva. We do *not* want to do anything that they would perceive as a sell-out of mutually held principles."[65] The White House would insist on vetoing a bill that had been passed by both chambers and on an agreement in advance that there be no override attempt. In addition, there would have to be an agreement with Bevill and Wright on the key elements of

---

[64] Letter to the president from Jim Wright, September 26, 1978, Jimmy Carter Library, Personal Secretary Handwriting File, Box 103, 9/27/78.

[65] Memorandum to the president from Jim McIntyre, Stu Eizenstat, Frank Moore, and Anne Wexler, "Public Works Veto Strategy," September 28, 1978, Jimmy Carter Library, Personal Secretary Handwriting File, Box 104, folder 9/29/78.

the compromise bill, which would be immediately passed by the House and the Senate. This course, it was argued, would avert the override fight, which would harm congressional relations and—in essential agreement with Jim Wright's analysis that the veto was interrelated with other congressional issues—inevitably affect a vote on natural gas deregulation. "If the compromise is successful, we will have taken a significant step toward putting behind us, for the balance of your Administration, confrontations with the Congress over the Water Resource issue." Carter

FIGURE 3. Jimmy Carter meets with Majority Leader Jim Wright and Tom Bevill at the Oval Office.

Source. Courtesy of the Jimmy Carter Library.
Note. Jimmy Carter met with Majority Leader Jim Wright (center) and Tom Bevill (D-AL) (left) at a meeting in the Oval Office in a bid to work out a compromise on the Energy and Water Appropriations Bill. Carter was dubious about the possibility of a compromise and efforts to defend his veto in Congress were already taking place. The men did not reach a compromise.

indicated his agreement with the approach noting on the memo, "Good—Proceed—(firmly)."[66]

The sides failed to reach a compromise agreement. As the attempt to reconcile positions was failing, Bevill requested another meeting with the president to further discuss the status of the impasse, but was rebuffed by the White House; Frank Moore told Bevill that the president's schedule was full and that he could not spare the time to meet with Bevill. In a final message of regret, Bevill wrote to the president:

> Mr. President, it is unfortunate that communication between the Administration and the Congress has not been better this year. Perhaps a great deal of the confusion about this bill could have been eliminated. Mr. President, it has always been the desire of my subcommittee to work with you in a reasonable way and in the best interest of our country, and we will continue to do so.[67]

Bevill enclosed a lengthy response to White House complaints about the bill. Several days later, in a meeting with the joint Democratic leadership at his routine Tuesday morning breakfast on October 3, the president indicated that significant differences remained between him and the water project proponents, and that he was likely to veto the bill the following day. He urged them to try to play down the effects of the veto on the aggressive agenda that was still facing Congress.

As the White House continued to move forward with the veto the next day, Gerald Rafshoon, the White House communications

---

[66] Memorandum to the president from Jim McIntyre, Stu Eizenstat, Frank Moore, and Anne Wexler, "Public Works Veto Strategy," September 28, 1978, Jimmy Carter Library, Personal Secretary Handwriting File, Box 104, folder 9/29/78.

[67] Letter to the president from Tom Bevill, September 27, 1978, *Tom Bevill Congressional Papers*, Box 6542, Folder 7.

FIGURE 4. A note sent by Jimmy Carter to members of Congress on the day he exercised his veto.

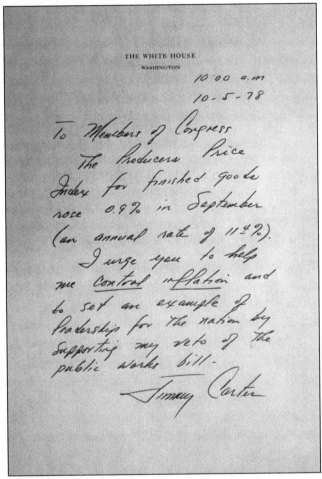

Source. Robert J. Lagomarsino Collection, California State University Channel Islands, Series 25, Box 1, Folder 14.
Note. On the day of the veto override vote in the House, Jimmy Carter sent notes to members of Congress highlighting the connection between water projects and inflation.

director, was tasked with the job of drafting a letter to all members of Congress that would accompany the president's veto message. Examining a first draft, Carter instructed Rafshoon via a handwritten comment to "[t]oughen it up = Emphasize inflation. Setting an example for the nation." Ultimately, the president's letter to Congress reflected these twin themes:

> At a time when all of us in the government are committed to fight inflation, we cannot afford to spend money where it is not really needed. By our actions, we in the government must set an example of restraint for the rest of the nation...only through constant sustained discipline can we achieve our shared objectives of restraining inflation, reducing the budget deficit, and making our government more efficient.[68]

And on October 5, 1978, the president officially returned the vetoed bill to the House and Senate. The stage was set for the end game.

WORKING TO SUSTAIN THE VETO

Laying the groundwork for sustaining the president's veto began months before he actually cast it. Waiting until Congress passed the bill to begin building momentum for sustaining it would not "be sufficient time to mount the campaign necessary to prevent an override."[69] The campaign involved both a *Hill strategy*—direct efforts to build a coalition of members of Congress in support of the veto—and a *public strategy* aimed at applying exter-

---

[68] Draft and final versions of "President's Letter to Every Senator and Member of Congress," Jimmy Carter Library, Personal Secretary Handwriting File.
[69] Memorandum for the president from Frank Moore, Anne Wexler, and Stu Eizenstat, "Energy and Water Development Appropriations Bill," September 21, 1978, Jimmy Carter Library Box 45, Public Works Appropriations [1].

nal pressure on members of Congress to support the veto. The public strategy involved gaining the support of interest groups that would advocate for the president's position, and a public relations blitz aimed at shaping public opinion by utilizing the media to broadcast the president's position on the water projects. The combination of internal and external pressure would help to overcome the formidable challenge of sustaining a veto of a bill that had passed with more than 300 votes.

At the core of the veto was the message that developed during the 1976 campaign and had carried through Carter's first confrontation with Congress over water projects: in balancing the budget, the place to begin was with wasteful congressional spending. Despite Carter's pro-environment stance, it was believed that environmental groups were fully aware of the environmental reasons for the veto, and that the conservative fiscal stance was more likely to win over pro-business interest groups and resonate with the public.

The Office of Congressional Liaison had learned a great deal from the battles that preceded the president's veto. The Hill strategy first focused on those House members who had voted with the administration on past water project votes, most notably the Derrick Amendment during the 1977 battle and the Edgar Amendment in 1978. According to a memo drafted by Jim Free, 133 members had voted with the administration in both instances and had "little reason not to vote to sustain the veto." However, he warned, "[I]f [a member] has projects in the bill, he probably has already received threats to have them deleted or he really believes in what we are trying to do and cannot be swayed by the other side." Derrick and Edgar had agreed in early September to lead the House effort. Additional members were designated for a task force that would work on colleagues to build support. Based on previous experience, the

Liaison Office recognized that Republican support would be necessary to sustain the veto; they enlisted Silvio Conte (MA), co-sponsor of the Derrick Amendment in 1977, and Republican Whip Robert Michel (IL) to build Republican support. Cabinet secretaries were to be directly involved in the effort by calling members of Congress with whom they had established a rapport to ask for support in the veto fight. It would be a difficult struggle, Free argued, because of the cards that Bevill and other members of the Appropriations Committee held: "The members advocating the Committee's position will lobby with the threat of discontinuing projects in a member's district or not starting any future projects in that district." This would make sustaining the veto more difficult than any previous effort that the Liaison Office had taken on in the past.[70]

Influencing public opinion required a full-court press involving the Offices of Public Liaison and Press Liaison, as well as key department secretaries. Following the first year of the administration, Jerry Rafshoon was added to the administration to revive the Office of Communications (Kumar 2007). Rafshoon joined the staff as Carter acknowledged that he was having difficulty communicating with the public. Despite unprecedented efforts to communicate through frequent press conferences and open town hall-style meetings, Carter admitted that his administration needed to improve its "ability to present the facts clearer to the American people through the press and vice versa" (quoted in Kumar 2007, 730). According to Rafshoon, "I was involved as an interpreter of [Carter's] policies, communicating the president's goals, trying to set the agenda, perceptions,

---

[70] Memorandum to Frank Moore from Jim Free, "Strategy for Possible Public Works Appropriations Bill Veto," September 11, 1978, Jimmy Carter Library, Office of Congressional Liaison, Box 45, Public Works Appropriations [1].

developing material for the president and other people on the White House staff and the cabinet to use in speeches and in selling [Carter's] programs."[71]

Rafshoon—a Carter confidante who did not become a formal member of the staff until July 1978—had earlier concluded that the administration was in need of "a little more know-how" in dealing with external constituencies (e.g., interest groups and the media). Anne Wexler, who had considerable Washington experience, joined the administration in 1978 as the director of the Office of Public Liaison. Her operation was organized into two parts: one focused on building "public support for" the president's "priority issues";[72] the other part was focused on outreach to groups and traditional Democratic constituencies. Wexler chaired the task force responsible for building public support for the president's position on water projects and public support for his veto. Generally speaking, these task forces formed in an ad hoc manner to focus administration resources on Carter's legislative and policy priorities.

In the case of the water projects, Wexler coordinated the efforts of the Office of Congressional Liaison and the Domestic Policy staff with the outreach efforts of the Offices of Public Liaison and Press Liaison. The Office of Congressional Liaison was responsible for identifying specific members of Congress who might be convinced to support the president's veto. According to Wexler, the cooperation of the liaison group was critical since "the congressional people [were] always coming back, re-looking at the [headcounts] saying 'well, we

[71] *Oral History Interview with Gerald Rafshoon*, Miller Center for Public Affairs Presidential Oral History Program, April 8, 1983, 5.

[72] Interview with Anne Wexler, August 2007, Washington, DC.

have got to focus more on X or Y,' because they were always doing congressional counts."[73] In response to this information, she claimed, "It was then our responsibility to bring thought-leaders and influentials from those districts into the White House for briefings."[74] In many cases, Wexler's group would go directly to the targeted member and ask, "'[W]ho do you think should be invited to the White House?' And they would get the credit for having people invited to the White House, which is a big deal."[75] The public strategy primarily centered on thirteen states in the East and Midwest where Moore and his staff thought many of the needed votes would come from. Orchestration of a pro-veto message in the press was the objective of the plan.

In an opening salvo in the Hill strategy, the White House hosted almost 200 House members to brief them on the president's concerns about the bill. House members left the briefings with an impressive packet of literature supporting the president's position, claiming that his policy was both fiscally sound while allowing for generous growth in water projects. It also included copies of seventeen editorials, mostly from major newspapers, endorsing the president's position in the water wars. A line from a *New York Newsday* editorial is representative of the sentiments expressed in the media:

> Carter has dropped plenty of hints that he wants to veto the bill and we hope he follows through. Not only does it provide funding for a number of highly dubious and expensive undertakings, but it pays scant attention

---

[73] Ibid.
[74] Ibid.
[75] Ibid.

to the water policy the administration announced last summer.[76]

Pat Bario of the Office of Press Liaison took the responsibility for inviting local press to the White House for briefings. On the water projects, it was often the case that reporters would meet directly with the president. According to Wexler, "[W]e got a lot of local press and the congressmen got the credit."[77] Public Liaison conducted ten briefing sessions for business, financial, taxpayer, and environmental groups who agreed to lobby about eighty members in support of the veto, as well as to issue endorsements of the veto when it was cast. The water projects united groups often opposed in Washington: "[I]n the case of the water projects it was the environmental interest groups and a lot of conservatives...who were interested in balanced budgets and fiscal conservatism." With these interest groups, the general approach was to invite them for "small briefings with the president, sometimes with the vice president...[the director of OMB] helped out a lot. We would lay out our case and then say 'here is our target list' and they did the rest. We couldn't say to them 'you are going to talk to Congressman X,' we didn't,"[78] but, possessed of the information, there is little doubt that groups would contact those members with whom they had friendly relationships. Outreach efforts also involved briefing public interest groups like the National Governors Association and the League of Cities on the administration's concerns. Jack Watson, whose primary responsibility was outreach to governors, convinced half a dozen governors to endorse the veto, and several Democratic governors were convinced to hold their criticisms of the

[76] *New York Newsday*, September 24, 1978.
[77] Interview with Anne Wexler, August 2007, Washington, DC.
[78] Ibid.

veto when the time came. In a larger effort, information was sent to more than 6,500 members of the media, resulting in a generally positive media environment.

As the "veto day" grew closer, the importance of winning the vote in the House became apparent. The original bill had overwhelming support in the Senate, and many senators had announced their intention to oppose President Carter's veto. Importantly, Democratic Leader Robert Byrd, who had worked tirelessly to pass the Carter agenda for almost two years, had indicated in public that he planned to break with the president on the veto vote. Without his help, it was unlikely that the president's veto would be sustained in the Senate. In a memo to Vice President Mondale, William Smith (Mondale's chief staffer in the Senate president's office) summed up the gloomy situation in the Senate: "We will have to win it in the House. Byrd has publicly vowed to fight for override in the Senate. It's his only public break with the President on a major issue and he's not likely to lose."[79]

On veto day, the public strategy focused on high-profile appearances of administration officials, governors, and party leaders across the country supporting the president's veto stance. Carter's case was, no doubt, boosted by laudatory editorials like the one that appeared in the *Los Angeles Times* the morning of the veto:

> We think the President has not only the right but also the duty to invoke the national interest in cases where he believes that regional interests have conspired to warp

---

[79] Memorandum for the vice president from Bill Smith, October 2, 1978, "Public Works Appropriation Veto—Status Report," *Walter F. Mondale Papers*, Vice Presidential Office: Files of the Administrative Assistant to the President of the Senate, Minnesota Historical Society (Location 154.J.8.10F Box 5).

the judgment of Congress about what constitutes money well spent. We hope the president's veto of this act is sustained, and that Congress will produce a new package of projects that more closely reflect the nation's real water needs.[80]

During Carter's first encounter with Congress over the water projects, the administration sent mixed messages to Congress. Carter was pulled in two different directions. On the one hand, he wanted to cooperate with the Democratic congressional leadership; he wanted to distinguish himself from the veto-happy Ford administration and promote the success of his other legislative priorities. On the other hand, Carter wanted to affect serious fiscal and environmental policy change. The decision to compromise betrayed his policy goals and confirmed to congressional leaders that he was without core beliefs—that he could be rolled. Maybe he was as gullible as members of Congress and the press had believed him to be, and as they had caricatured the "Georgia Mafia." The second battle in the water wars differed in that the Carter White House repeatedly and clearly signaled its intention to veto legislation inconsistent with its policy concerns. And this time, the White House had developed a strategy to sustain the veto by marshaling the necessary public and congressional support. The question remained, however, whether Carter would be able to exercise enough influence to sustain his veto.

---

[80] "The Pork Barrel Runneth Over," *Los Angeles Times*, October 4, 1978, morning edition.

CHAPTER 4

PRESIDENTIAL INFLUENCE IN CONGRESS

I learned the hard way that there was no party loyalty or discipline when a complicated or controversial issue was at stake—none. Each legislator had to be wooed and won individually. It was every member for himself, and the devil take the hindmost.

—Jimmy Carter (1995, 84)

...if the Chairman of the Appropriations Committee is talking to a member, and you're talking with the member, guess who's going to win...

—Frank Moore[1]

---

[1] *Oral History Interview with Frank Moore,* Jimmy Carter Library and Museum, July 30–31, 2002, 76.

In this chapter, we examine presidential influence within Congress quantitatively. The battle over water projects provides an opportunity to gauge the influence of the president on a highly salient piece of legislation in the face of a well-organized and powerful opposition. On one side was a president seeking to sustain a veto. Using the power and offices of the presidency, the White House mounted a major campaign to influence members of Congress to shape the political context within which members of Congress decide. On the other side of the battle were several powerful members of Congress in positions to either ply supporters with future policy favors or punish them by failing to support future requests. Furthermore, because of their status as members, they had direct and mostly unfettered access to their colleagues. What they lacked was the ability to effectively shape the external context.

We employ vote counts from multiple sources to describe and explain the competition between the president and members of Congress over this important veto. Vote counts performed by the Office of Congressional Liaison are used to describe the Carter administration's congressional strategy for sustaining the president's veto in Congress. Using data regarding which members of Congress the president personally lobbied, we can estimate the success of President Carter's lobbying effort. We also employ vote-count data from the congressional papers of Representative Tom Bevill (D-AL), chairman of the House Appropriations Subcommittee on Energy and Water, and of Senator John Stennis (D-MS), chairman of the Senate Appropriations Subcommittee on Public Works, both of whom were working inside of Congress to override the Carter veto. Taken together, these data will provide unique insight into the relationship between Carter and the Democratic Congress.

In the first section of this chapter, we develop a framework aimed at understanding the general elements of coalition building in Congress. We then turn to a description of the results of an analysis of the headcount data from the Carter White House and from Bevill's efforts to lobby House members. We conclude by evaluating our framework in a multivariate context.

BUILDING COALITIONS IN CONGRESS: A FRAMEWORK

Both sides in a legislative battle begin the fight with core supporters—members of Congress who can be counted on to support their position. The composition of the core support group varies from issue to issue. On any given issue, core support may be a function of partisanship, but it may also reflect policy differences, regional splits, ideological conflicts, committee loyalties, future political calculations, and even personal attachments. Many members of Congress, perhaps most on the majority of issues, may be persuaded to join one or the other side in a legislative battle. It is the job of coalition builders to identify these "pursuadables" and convert them into supporters.

The coalition-building process inside Congress takes place within an "opinion context." Depending on the political issue at hand, the public may be taking an intense interest or may have little interest. Both sides of a legislative fight compete to define the opinion context by "framing" the issue for the public. Issue framing centers on shaping how the public understands a policy issue. An extensive literature has developed that examines issue framing. Harris (2007) summarized the literature and identified four types of issue frames used by political leaders. *Causal frames* offer theories for social problems and imply policy solutions. *Group-centric frames* seek to influence public perceptions of "who wins and who loses," given a specific policy response. *Episodic frames* underlie attempts to frame issues as "us versus them" battles by focusing on specific individual cases. *Conflict*

FIGURE 5. A coalition-building framework.

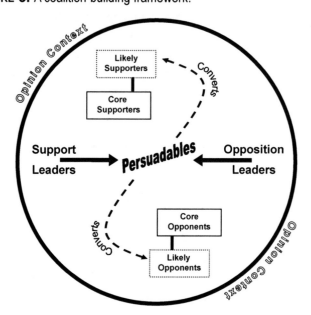

Note. The challenge facing those seeking to build a coalition in Congress is transforming persuadable members into likely supporters. The conversion process occurs within a broader opinion context. Depending on the degree of public attention, and the tenor of public opinion, it may be easier for one side to persuade supporters to join a coalition.

frames are characterized by the use of "wedge issues" that attempt to split existing coalitions between political supporters and the legislative parties. By employing issue frames, political actors seek to influence public support for their preferred policies.

Competition to frame issues is particularly intense when an issue involves matters that activate powerful economic and/or social lobbies, involve questions of intense interest to the public, and generate substantial attention in the media. Interest groups may play a central role in the battle to frame issues. It is common, on issues that are highly contested, for both sides in a legislative battle to build coalitions with outside groups that have shared interests. These interest groups are able to use their substantial resources to develop and amplify issue frames that activate their membership and help to shape the public opinion context.[2]

The opinion context can make it easier or harder for each side to convert members of Congress who are possible supporters, that is, those who are not core supporters of either side, whom we call "pursuadables." In the case of the water projects, the administration sought to define the battle as an attempt to rein in wasteful congressional spending, balance the budget, and reduce inflationary pressures. Congress, they argued, was pursuing its narrow and short-term political interests over the national interest. The administration also framed the water projects in environmental terms, arguing that the projects were environmentally harmful. In essence, the White House and its interest group allies (business groups—see chapter 3) employed a causal frame to shape public understanding of the battle over the water projects. Members of Congress who supported the water projects sought to define the battle in institutional terms: President Carter, they argued, was attempting to usurp the congressional power of the purse; a vote for the override was a vote to protect congressional prerogative. To the degree that one issue frame dominates in the opinion context, it would advantage one side and disadvantage the other. The frame provided by the White House was intuitive and powerful. It focused public attention on the generally accepted proposition that politicians (especially members of Congress) are primarily interested in promoting their narrow self-interest, and it argued that defeating the water projects served broader collective interests, both economic and

---

[2] See, for instance, Browne (1998) and Goldstein (1999).

environmental. As we have discussed, the White House built a large and powerful coalition of interest groups, and skillfully employed the media to shape the opinion context, thereby making it difficult for members of Congress—especially those with a natural tendency to support Carter's efforts—to support a veto override.

RESULTS

Table 1 illustrates the results of three key votes on the Energy and Water Appropriations Bill. First, consider column one, which displays support in Congress for the president's position on the Edgar Amendment; the amendment would have removed from the bill the nine objectionable water projects that had been removed by the O'Neill–Carter compromise from the FY 1978 Bill. Despite the president's veto threat and his strong endorsement of the Edgar Amendment, it lost badly, with the president's position failing to gain majority support from significant groups within Congress. The strongest source of support in Congress was from the junior members of Congress; a majority of the Watergate babies and a near-majority of first-term members were among the most supportive of the president. These junior members did not have significant projects in their districts included in the bill. But it goes beyond that, since there were members who did have important projects, including Butler Derrick—one of Carter's chief allies in the House. It is just as likely that many of these members were representing changing public opinion on budget deficits and federal spending, and responding to those changes through their votes. In fact, many of these members were elected by promising to "change the way that business is done in Washington," and this was one way to illustrate that commitment to their constituents. Fortunately for the president, there were many new members

TABLE 1. Key votes on the Energy and Water Development Appropriations Bill by subgroups within the House.

	Edgar Amendment % Voting *Yes* with Carter	Final Passage % Voting *No* with Carter	Veto Override % Voting *No* with Carter
Electoral Status			
Frosh	45.8 (33)	18.1 (13)	52.2 (36)
Class of 1974	52.3 (46)	23.9 (21)	65.5 (55)
Region			
Northeast	48.6 (52)	15.9 (17)	59.0 (59)
Midwest	45.9 (56)	21.3 (26)	61.1 (69)
Border	33.3 (12)	3.0 (1)	25.0 (8)
South	21.2 (7)	9.9 (10)	3.2 (1)
West	13.2 (10)	6.6 (5)	32.4 (23)
Party			
Democrats	33.2 (97)	12.7 (37)	46.0 (125)
Republicans	30.6 (45)	15.0 (22)	45.9 (62)
Ideology[a]			
Carter Supporter	48.6 (68)	46.6 (27)	40.3 (75)
Carter Moderate	27.9 (39)	25.9 (15)	30.1 (56)
Carter Opponent	23.6 (33)	27.6 (16)	29.6 (55)
Electoral[b]			
Marginal	42.3 (30)	21.1 (15)	58.8 (40)
Non-Marginal	31.8 (111)	12.6 (44)	44.0 (144)
Committees			
Appropriations	17.9 (10)	7.1 (4)	22.6 (12)
Public Works	15.6 (7)	6.7 (3)	25.0 (11)
Energy & Commerce	48.8 (21)	18.6 (8)	66.7 (28)
Budget	36.0 (9)	32.0 (8)	62.5 (15)

Note. Percentages are the percent of that group voting with the president. Numbers in parentheses are the number of House members voting to support the president's position.
[a] Ideological categories are based on members' absolute proximity to the president based on Poole and Rosenthal nominate scores. *Supporters* are those within one standard deviation of the president, *moderates* are between one and two standard deviations, and *opponents* are more than two standard deviations from the president. [b] Marginal members received 55% or less of the district vote in the previous election.

in the House; however, there were not enough to win on this amendment.

The results on this vote also indicate a regional split on the Edgar Amendment. While near-majorities of the northeastern and midwestern delegations were supportive of the president's position, House members from the southern, border, and western states defected from it. The defections of southern and border state representatives are somewhat surprising, given the shared roots of the president and many of these members. The southern

FIGURE 6. Regional distribution of support for Carter on the Edgar Amendment.

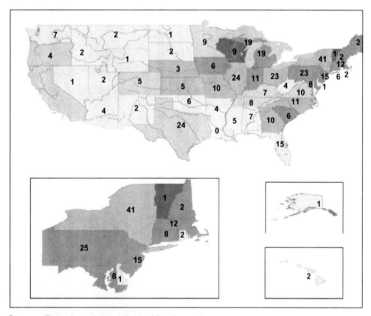

Source. Based on data collected by the authors.
Note. Darker shading indicates the level of support for the president's position in the state. Numbers indicate the number of House members from that state.

states were the foundation for Carter's electoral coalition and his capture of the presidency; inside and outside of Congress, Carter's win was a source of pride for many southerners, who often doubted that a "true southerner" could win the presidency due to the history of the Civil War, segregation, and the Civil Rights battles of the 1950s and '60s. Still, southern resistance of the president's position was not surprising since many of the projects in the bill benefited southern states and districts, and the most powerful members of the Appropriations Committee were from the South and were leading the fight to reinstate these projects.

Resistance from the West is also not surprising. Many western states rely on federal water projects to bring water to arid lands for farming, to provide energy through hydroelectric projects, and to supply critical water to cities and towns. Figure 6 graphically illustrates the nature and degree of the geographic split. House members from the Northeast and Midwest generally provided more support for the Edgar Amendment and Carter than did members from the South, though considerable support did come from the South. The farther west the state, however, the less support Edgar and Carter could count on. During a period when the West was experiencing drought conditions, western legislators were loathe to support cuts in water projects, and Carter's efforts were successfully portrayed by western politicians—most importantly Ronald Reagan—as a "war on the West," adding tinder to the intensifying "sagebrush rebellion." Ronald Reagan took up the "war on the West" battle cry, which helped him to win support in the West and cruise to victory in 1980.[3]

---

[3] Of course, this was but one of several elements of the Republican critique of Carter. The Iranian Hostage Crisis (November 4, 1979, to January 20, 1981) provided support for the narrative that portrayed Carter as weak and indecisive, and the Panama Canal Treaties (1977–1978) provided grist for a narrative

When the vote is broken down by party, it is apparent that there was little difference between Democrats and Republicans. This was not a partisan vote, one in which the president could count on extraordinary support from his Democratic partisans; 33.2% of Democrats and 30.6% of Republicans supported the president's position on the amendment. An area where the president found support was from marginal members of the House, those elected with 55% or less of the two-party vote in their districts. Though the support was not overwhelming, 42.3% of marginal members supported the president, compared to 31.8% of the non-marginal members. Since the vast majority of members were not marginal, the percentage difference did not translate into a huge number of votes for the president.

Finally, when we look at committee support for the president, we see dramatic differences across committees. Members of the Appropriations Committee and the Public Works Committee were the least supportive of the president's position. The Public Works Committee was the committee that authorized the vast majority of the water projects contained in the bill, and it was the work of the Appropriations Committee that was being challenged by the amendment. Jim Wright, the majority leader and a member of the Public Works Committee, was one of the staunchest defenders of the bill, and Tom Bevill, the subcommittee chair who wrote the bill, was advocating against the amendment. With such prominent members closely watching the votes of their committee colleagues, committee members would be unwilling to buck their leadership (even if they were so disposed). So, as might be expected, members of these

that suggested that Carter was selling out American national security (Clymer 2008).

committees voted overwhelmingly against the Edgar Amendment. It is worth noting that Edgar was a member of the Public Works Committee and one of the few members of that committee to advocate against many of the projects that were authorized by his committee.

Results for members of the Energy and Commerce and Budget Committees are different. While not achieving majority support within these committees, presidential support was higher. Energy and Commerce had jurisdiction over the authorized projects that are often included in this particular bill, but the committee had not yet passed its authorization bill for FY 1979; members of Energy and Commerce objected to the appropriations process moving forward in the absence of an authorizing bill. In a joint letter, Energy and Commerce Chair Harley O. Staggers (D-WV), Ranking Democrat John Dingell (MI), and Ranking Republican Clarence Brown (OH) had urged defeat of the Rule accompanying HR 12928, which ruled authorization-related amendments out of order.[4] Citing similar past problems, Appropriations Chair George Mahon responded that "[i]f the Appropriations Committee had waited for these authorizations, the development of our nation's energy programs would have been seriously delayed." He continued, perhaps a bit condescendingly, "[T]he only real solution I know to these very serious problems is for the authorization committees to begin reporting two-year authorizations, or authorizations at least a year in advance."[5] Despite the jurisdictional battle inside Congress, the president had generally praised the energy portion of the bill (which, as Mahon had pointed out to Dingell,

---

[4] "Dear Colleague," from Staggers, Dingell, and Brown, June 14, 1978, *Tom Bevill Congressional Papers*, Box 6542, Folder 8.
[5] Letter from George Mahon to John Dingell, June 6, 1978, *Tom Bevill Congressional Papers*, Box 6542, Folder 8.

closely approximated the authorizations contained in his pending subcommittee bill); none of the projects authorized by Energy and Commerce were threatened by the amendment, so these members may have felt they had more leeway (even a reason) to cast a vote with the president. Because of the jurisdiction of the Budget Committee—with responsibility for developing a blueprint for the congressional budget, and their commitment to budget restraint—committee members would likely be sympathetic to the president's position to slash "wasteful" spending. And the increased support (31.8%) of the committee's members reflects that willingness to vote in favor of an amendment that was opposed by many powerful House members.

Despite President Carter's support for the Edgar Amendment, his open opposition to the bill, and his veto threat, the bill was victorious on final passage. The vote on final passage seemed to indicate significant support for the congressional position over the president's position: 263 in favor and fifty-nine against (with 108 members not voting and four announced "yes" votes). Analysis of support for the president's position on final passage in the House reveals similar patterns as with the Edgar Amendment (see Table 1). The president's position lost support among almost all of the groups included in the analysis (except southern members); eight of the nine members who had supported the president on the Edgar Amendment held tough with the president on final passage.

While the vote on final passage did not provide a veto-proof margin, supporters of the bill were only twenty-seven votes from the two-thirds necessary to override the veto (290 votes), and the president was almost eighty votes short of the 145 necessary to sustain it. When combined with the final votes on the conference report, the president's position looked pretty grim; the president had threatened a veto of an important bill, and the Congress had snubbed him by overwhelmingly approving the conference report and sending the bill to his desk for a signature. As the end of FY 1978 loomed, failure to sign the appropriations bill would create some havoc in those parts of government that relied on the funding it contained. Furthermore, by late September 1978, members of Congress were focused on the upcoming midterm elections—especially Democrats—who were fully aware that the majority party typically loses seats in midterm elections, and with a fairly unpopular president (with an approval rating in the mid- to upper 40% range), some of their members were in tight battles. Overriding the president's veto would avoid a partial fiscal crisis, show them standing up to a somewhat unpopular president, and get them back to their districts for the last month of the campaign.

At this point, we are able to take stock of the tactical situation in the House. Using these two votes, we can determine the nature of Carter's core supporters and core opponents. Those who voted for the Edgar Amendment to strip the water projects and voted against the appropriations bill are considered core supporters of Carter. Those who voted against the Edgar Amendment and for the appropriations bill are considered core opponents of Carter. Other members are considered persuadable. Among the persuadables are those who voted on the two motions in contradictory ways ("yes" on Edgar and "yes" on final passage, "no" on Edgar and "no" on final passage), and those for whom there is not a complete voting history on both votes. Carter could count on the unwavering support of only fifty-one House members, compared to 191 who would be considered core opponents, that is, those who would likely vote to override the president's veto. Working in favor of the president—and likely making the override proponents feel dyspeptic—was the fact that 192 members fell into the persuadable category. In short, a great deal of uncertainty surrounded the override vote. And there is some reason to believe that uncertainty, in this case, favored the Carter forces. For many members, voting to sustain the veto could be interpreted by their constituents as support for fiscal discipline and a vote against wasteful spending (rather than support for the president); the implications for government finance would probably be unnoticed by their constituents. The vote of a conference report can often be a "hurrah vote" with little to no incentive for a no-vote that will please very few of the more senior members of Congress on a bill that is destined to pass. In short, votes on the conference report might be viewed as somewhat "insincere." On final House passage, many members had not voted, leaving their true preferences somewhat in doubt. And with a tireless effort on the part of the entire White House, the groundwork might be laid for sustaining the veto.

As the third column of Table 1 indicates, President Carter did make significant inroads into some groups in support of his veto. As Carter suggested, on this vote partisanship was not the foundation on which his victory would be built. He gained votes at the same rate from both Democrats and Republicans (46% and 45%, respectively). As suggested by Frank Moore in his memo to the president, the greatest gains in support of the president's position came from less senior members, as well as among members from the Northeast and the Midwest. Carter gained 52% support from first-term members and almost two-thirds support from the Watergate babies—impressive gains within both groups. Also impressive were gains among members from the Northeast. Fifty-nine percent of these members supported the president on the override, compared to 48.6% on the Edgar Amendment and only 15.9% on House passage. Gains among Midwest members were similar; Carter gained 61.1% of the Midwest members, compared to 45.9% for Edgar and 21.3%

on House passage. Marginal members, perhaps responding to the White House public relations strategy and reaction from constituents, heavily supported the president (58.8%). Gains among Energy and Commerce and Budget Committee members improved substantially, increasing from 48.8% to 66.7% and 36% to 62.5%, respectively. What was perhaps a little more surprising were the president's gains, small as they might be, among members of the Appropriations and Public Works Committees. While the total number of votes gained by the president was only six, these were likely the six most difficult votes to achieve, given the watchful eyes of the powerful men associated with these committees.

THE OVERRIDE BATTLE FROM THE INSIDE

Dear Mr. President,

Congratulations on your "stunning" victory. I have never seen a finer orchestrated movement. Most of the credit goes to Jim Free. We are fortunate that he is on our side.

Best wishes,
Butler.[6]

Through closer examination of Carter's "stunning" victory, we seek to shed some light on how this victory was achieved, and on the means and ability of presidents to influence congressional outcomes. To do this, we employ vote counts and qualitative data from inside Carter's Office of Congressional Liaison, the president's own notes while seeking support from members of Congress, and vote counts and strategy information from within

---

[6] Handwritten letter to President Carter from Butler Derrick (D-SC), October 6, 1978, Jimmy Carter Library, Name File, Derrick, Butler, 1/20/77–10/27/78.

the office of Representative Tom Bevill, who led the fight to override the president's veto. By combining these data sources, we can estimate the lengths and limitations of the persuasive powers of a president. Such an examination also provides some insight into the critical work of the liaison's office, so rarely the subject of systematic analysis.

Leading the fight for the president in the House was Frank Moore, head of the office, but his chief House liaison was Jim Free who, along with other staff, was charged with lobbying members on behalf of the president's position. By continuously monitoring individual members and their propensity to vote with or against the president, Moore and Free could make informed decisions about how the president's scarcest resource, time, would be used to directly lobby members on behalf of his veto through White House meetings and telephone calls. Using records of the president's attempts to influence members directly, we can estimate how many votes the president was able to influence through personal contact with a member. A personal phone call could be effective in a number of ways: (1) it can emphasize the weightiness of the decision that a member will make, (2) it can convince the member of the president's commitment to a particular position, and (3) it can allow the president to make his case to a member who may be getting heavily skewed information coming from senior House leaders. In short, a presidential phone call has the possibility of being an effective tool for maintaining or converting a member. Given the president's limited time, calls should focus on those members who are most likely to change position.

Free and Moore recommended calls to sixty-seven House members to discuss the vote, according to White House documents. This is a small number of calls compared to the number of members in the House (15.4%), but it is important to remember the strategic position of the president on an override vote: he needed only 144 votes to sustain the veto. Based on the votes for final passage, Carter needed about eighty votes, so sixty-seven calls could go a long way toward rounding them up. Of the sixty-seven calls, forty were to members who had voted "yes" on House passage of the bill, twenty-two were to members who did not vote on passage, four were to members who voted "no" on passage, and one was to a member who was an announced "yes." On a percentage basis, the greatest proportion of calls went to those not voting (20.4%) and those who voted "yes" (15.2%).

For his part, Tom Bevill contacted eighty-five members, a slightly larger percentage of the House membership (19.5%). For Bevill's part, the job must have seemed initially easier since he needed fewer votes to override the president's veto based on support for his bill on House passage. Unlike Carter, who contacted few of his supporters on passage, the greatest number of Bevill's contacts was with members who voted with him on passage (45), more than half of his eighty-five contacts. Given that Bevill began from what seemed to be a position of strength (a base of 192 votes), maintaining the foundation of his coalition made sense. Conversions would be a second priority, with Bevill contacting twenty-five members who did not vote on final passage. This would seem fertile ground for Bevill since some of the nonvoting members likely "took a walk," that is, they purposely did not vote at the request of Bevill to enhance the size of the margin on final passage so that Bevill could send a strong message to the president that the latter should not attempt a veto. Finally, Bevill approached only thirteen members who voted "no" on final passage. No-voters would be the most difficult to convert since they had stuck with the president on the Edgar Amendment and the vote on final passage, but clearly Bevill believed that he could find some supporters among these members.

It is interesting to compare on whom the two men were focusing in the House when attempting to marshal votes. Table 2 breaks down the two men's contacts according to the same classification used in Table 1. For the most part, the whipping strategy employed on both sides was remarkably similar. More than 40% of both men's contacts were freshmen and sophomore members, with Bevill contacting a higher proportion of sophomore members (22.4%) in his target group than Carter (17.9%). Regionally, both men heavily focused their efforts on the northeastern and midwestern states, while Carter also focused significant effort on the border states (28.4% of contacts) and some on the West (13.4% of contacts). Most of the lobby effort on both sides was placed on Democrats, with Bevill making something of an additional effort with Republicans. This should not be interpreted as the president and his advisers ignoring the Republicans; the strategy laid out by Moore and Free rested heavily on Republican support, and they had enlisted two Republicans to whip votes on the president's behalf. Finally, in terms of committees, members of Public Works, as well as Energy and Commerce, got the most attention from the president, while Bevill focused primarily on Energy and Commerce. The reason that Bevill likely focused on Energy and Commerce was that many of their projects were funded by the appropriations bill; he likely focused on the implications of a veto for funding of projects of interest to those members.

The vote counts provide us with an opportunity to assess the relative vote counting of the two sides. By examining how each side *believed* members would vote versus how they *actually* voted, we can gain insight into the ability of each side to predict the outcome of the vote and see whether there are areas in which the two sides were most likely to misidentify votes. Table 3 compares the White House vote count to the vote on the override. Heading into

TABLE 2. Jimmy Carter's and Tom Bevill's lobbying activity on the House override vote by subgroup.

	Number and % Contacted by Carter	Number and % Contacted by Bevill
Electoral Status		
Frosh	16 (23.8%)	21 (24.7)
Class of 1974	12 (17.9)	19 (22.4)
Region		
Northeast	15 (22.4)	33 (38.8)
Midwest	20 (29.9)	31 (36.5)
Border	19 (28.4)	6 (7.1)
South	4 (5.9)	9 (10.6)
West	9 (13.4)	6 (7.1)
Party		
Democrats	49 (73.1)	58 (68.2)
Republicans	18 (26.9)	27 (31.8)
Ideology[a]		
Carter Supporter	18 (27.7)	33 (39.3)
Carter Moderate	26 (40.0)	30 (35.7)
Carter Opponent	21 (32.3)	21 (25.0)
Electoral[b]		
Marginal	13 (19.4)	19 (22.4)
Non-Marginal	52 (77.6)	65 (76.5)
Committees		
Appropriations	6 (8.9)	5 (5.9)
Public Works	9 (13.4)	6 (7.1)
Energy & Commerce	7 (10.4)	10 (11.8)
Budget	4 (5.9)	5 (5.9)

Note. Numbers in parentheses are percentages. Percentages represent the proportion that group contacted by Carter or Bevill.
[a] Ideological categories are based on members' absolute proximity to the president based on Poole and Rosenthal nominate scores. *Supporters* are those within one standard deviation of the president, *moderates* are between one and two standard deviations, and *opponents* are more than two standard deviations from the president. [b] Marginal members received 55% or less of the district vote in the previous election.

the vote, the White House vote count—as of October 4, the evening before the vote—was projecting at least 154 votes against the override (combining the "no" and "leaning no" categories) and thus could conclude with some confidence that they would surpass the number of votes necessary to sustain the president's veto (144), though it might be close with only a ten-vote margin. Looking at those members who said they planned to vote "no" and did vote "no" (dark gray box in lower right corner), the count was about 87% accurate, with only 11% unexpectedly voting "yes"; the count was 63% accurate with regard to those "leaning no," with 37% of those members unexpectedly voting "yes" on the override (upper right corner). Comparing this record to that of those members whom the White House expected to vote "yes" (upper left corner), we see that the vote count was slightly more accurate, with 77.9% of those who indicated a "yes" vote and 89.5% of those "leaning yes" voted for the override; the level of defection from this position to support the president on the vote was a bit lower, 18.8% and 10.5%, respectively (lower left corner). As of the evening before the vote, more than 100 votes were unknown or undecided, leaving substantial uncertainty about the final vote. Overall, the White House count could be judged as conservative, but their analysis must have led them to believe that the president's veto would be sustained. In fact, there must have been some sense of delight in the Liaison Office that Bevill would need to convert all of his supporters to a "yes" position, along with the vast majority of the unknown votes to his position, to successfully override the president's veto.

Bevill's count indicated that he could count on 247 votes to override the president's veto (the combined total of the "yes" and "leaning yes" columns), with a large number of votes (158) still unknown. The addition of forty-three votes, minus any of those who might "take a walk," would bring victory based on this

TABLE 3. White House vote count and the House override vote.

| | White House Vote Count | | | | | | |
	Yes	Leaning Yes	Undecided	Unknown	Leaning No	No	Row Totals
Override Vote							
Yes	116 (77.9)	17 (89.5)	14 (32.6)	52 (76.5)	10 (37.0)	14 (11.0)	223
P-Y	2 (1.3)	–	–	3 (4.4)	–	–	5
A-Y	–	–	1 (2.3)	–	–	1 (.8)	2
P-N	–	–	–	2 (2.9)	–	1 (.8)	3
No	28 (18.8)	2 (10.5)	25 (58.1)	8 (11.8)	17 (63.0)	110 (86.6)	190
NV	3 (2.0)	–	3 (7.0)	2 (2.9)	–	1 (.8)	9
Col. Totals	149	19	43	68	27	127	

Note. P-Y = Paired *Yes.* A-Y = Announced *Yes.* P-N = Paired *No.* NV = Not voting.
χ^2 = 210.10 (*p* < .000). λ = .54 (*p* < .000).

TABLE 4. Tom Bevill's vote count and the House override vote.

| | Tom Bevill Vote Count | | | | | | |
	Yes	Leaning Yes	Undecided	Unknown	Leaning No	No	Row Totals
Override Vote							
Yes	159 (71.6)	9 (36.0)	7 (23.3)	46 (35.9)	2 (18.0)	–	223
P-Y	2 (.9)	1 (4.0)	–	2 (1.6)	–	–	5
A-Y	1 (.5)	–	–	1 (.8)	–	–	2
P-N	1 (.5)	–	1 (3.3)	1 (.8)	–	–	3
No	55 (24.8)	15 (60.0)	22 (73.3)	66 (51.6)	9 (81.8)	23 (100)	190
NV	4 (1.8)	–	–	5 (3.9)	–	–	9
Col. Totals	222	25	30	128	11	23	

Note. P-Y = Paired Yes. A-Y = Announced Yes. P-N = Paired No. NV = Not voting.
χ^2 = 120.65 (p < .000). λ = .33 (p < .000).

TABLE 5. Comparing the two vote counts.

White House Vote Count	Tom Bevill Vote Count						Row Totals
	Yes	Leaning Yes	Undecided	Unknown	Leaning No	No	
Yes	95 (42.8)	9 (36.0)	5 (16.7)	38 (31.1)	2 (18.2)	–	223
Lean Yes	14 (6.3)	1 (4.0)	–	3 (2.5)	1 (9.1)	–	5
UD	17 (7.7)	6 (24.0)	2 (6.7)	15 (12.3)	–	3 (13.0)	2
UK	52 (23.4)	1 (4.0)	2 (6.7)	12 (9.8)	1 (9.1)	–	3
Lean No	9 (4.1)	1 (4.0)	15 (50.0)	9 (7.4)	1 (9.1)	1 (4.3)	190
No	35 (15.8)	7 (28.0)	2 (6.7)	45 (36.9)	6 (54.5)	19 (82.6)	9
Col. Totals	222	25	30	122	11	23	

Note. UD = Undecided. UK = Unknown.
$\chi^2 = 106.31$ ($p < .000$). $\lambda = .14$ ($p < .000$).

count. As Table 3 indicates, Bevill's count was much more optimistic than the White House count. Almost 25% of those whom Bevill was counting as "yes" votes voted "no," and 60% of those "leaning yes" voted "no." While Bevill was quite successful at identifying those members who were sure to vote against him, he lost the majority (55.7%) of the votes that were classified as "undecided" or "unknown." Bevill's count, by contrast to the White House count, could be called optimistic; there must have been some sentiment on the part of Bevill, his supporters, and staff that they would likely override the president's veto.

The nature of these two counts comes into high relief when they are directly compared. Table 5 compares how each member was classified according to the Bevill count and the White House count. If both sides were getting the same answers from members, most of the cases would fall on the diagonal, that is, in the boxes shaded gray. Close inspection of these cells indicates that the two sides agreed on only 130 of the votes that were in play. Furthermore, focusing on those votes in the four cells inside the dark lines, among those that were "unknown" or "undecided" according to Bevill, the White House had established that these were votes for the president's position.

This analytical exercise suggests that the White House count was more accurate overall. That this is the case suggests the relative strengths of the White House, even when it is lobbying against powerful forces within Congress. First, the White House has more resources to dedicate to such an effort. From all indications, the Office of Congressional Liaison was almost fully dedicated to the task of sustaining the president's veto with several staff members working the phones and analyzing the votes. This contrasts with the resources of someone like Representative Bevill, a single member of Congress who has his staff and the efforts of his allies and their staff—all of whom must continue to perform their other functions in addition to working to override the veto. Members also have more incentive to remain uncommitted when responding to their congressional colleagues. They know that they would likely have to work with Bevill on future votes and approach him on future projects. By staying uncommitted, they can make a "game time" decision; as the votes are being registered, they can cast the vote that best serves their future interests. If they can vote with Bevill without hurting the president (once the vote tally has shown that the president's veto was sustained), then they will remain in his good graces; if they defect once the cause is lost, then they can argue to Bevill that their vote was necessary to respond to both constituent concerns and an impending election; they could claim that their vote was Bevill's if it was necessary.

THE TOOLS OF INFLUENCE

Carter used a variety of approaches to influence members' votes. In some cases, members of Congress simply wanted to be asked for their support; they reveled in a call from the White House and the president asking for their help. In other cases, more creative persuasion was necessary. Often, the president focused on past support for his positions and the importance of the vote for the remainder of the presidency. With many of the Republicans that were contacted, the president tried to convince them that their help was needed "to stop wasteful government spending," a favorite refrain of many of the Republican members.[7]

Carter often tied issues together in interesting ways. Sidney Yates (D-IL), a Jewish-American, was a powerful member of the

---

[7] Memorandum to the president from Frank Moore, "To Ask Their Support in Sustaining Veto," October 4, 1978, Jimmy Carter Library, Office of Congressional Liaison, Box 45, Public Works Appropriations [1].

FIGURE 7. Presidential call sheet and notes for telephone calls to House members.

THE WHITE HOUSE

WASHINGTON

CONGRESSIONAL TELEPHONE CALLS

TO: Sid Yates (D-Ill), Floyd Fithian (D-Ind), Jim Collins (R-Tx), John Buchanan (R-Ala), Ike Skelton (D-Mo), Ron Mazzoli (D-Ky), Jim Leach (R-Iowa), Adam Benjamin (D-Ind), George Danielson (D-Cal)

DATE: October 4, 1978

RECOMMENDED BY: Frank Moore F.M./BR

PURPOSE: To ask their support on the public works veto.

TOPICS OF DISCUSSION: As follow.

None of the following Members have projected appearances by senior Administration officials. We have noted previous appearances below for Fithian and Mazzoli.

5 Finally agreed to recheck data ē staff

Sid Yates. Has been with us in the past. This is important to me to continue to be able to provide the leadership necessary to reach a successful conclusion of the Peace Talks. against Perkins – Voted ē Edgar = Brainwashed - Sounds like Bevill & Wright

Prob 2 Lafayette Lake wants to kill

Floyd Fithian. You were successful with him yesterday on the rule on energy. He is not with us now. He generally responds to economy and good government-type issues. Chip attended Fithian's major fundraiser in Indiana in June (a boat trip for his sponsors' club). Jim Free call tomorrow

1

Jim Collins. He has been consistently with us in the past on water policy. He responds to fiscal conservative issues -- avoid the natural gas issue.

3 *

John Buchanan. John just survived a tough primary attack from the right. He has been with us on most foreign policy issues and should stay with us. Bevill is prob. "Will take another look" (with us on nat gas)

Source. Courtesy of the Jimmy Carter Library and Museum.

Note. This call sheet was used by President Carter to make notes about his discussions with the members and make notes about how likely they were to support his position.

Appropriations Committee. In an attempt to garner his support, Carter linked the vote to the ongoing Middle East peace initiative: "This is important to me to continue to be able to provide the leadership necessary to reach a successful conclusion of the Peace Talks."[8] President Carter must have been taken aback by Yates' initial negative response; he noted next to Yates' name: "[A]gainst Perkins = voted with Edgar = Brainwashed – Sounds like Bevill & Wright." Later in the conversation, Carter noted a shift in Yates' position—marking him down as a probable "no," writing, "Finally agreed to recheck data with staff."[9]

President Carter and his advisers were unable, in this case, to direct substantive benefits to a member of Congress in order to curry favor with the member. It would have been contradictory to argue against pork while gaining votes by offering pork projects to members; such behavior would have alienated core supporters, and override opponents would have illustrated, with glee, how the White House opposed congressional pork but was willing to offer *White House* pork. Frank Moore said of the practice of "buying votes" in Congress: "[W]e never did that. I mean generally you tried to have good relations with [members]—you never did that."[10] As Moore mentioned, the president had few substantive benefits that he could offer to members to "buy" their votes, though the president and his allies could appeal to

---

[8] Memorandum to the president from Frank Moore, "To Ask Their Support in Sustaining Veto," October 4, 1978, Jimmy Carter Library, Office of Congressional Liaison, Box 45, Public Works Appropriations [1].

[9] Memorandum to the president from Frank Moore, "To Ask Their Support of the Public Works Veto," October 4, 1978, Jimmy Carter Library, Personal Secretary Handwriting File, Box 105, 10/5/78.

[10] There is reason to believe that, on other votes, the administration did use projects to garner votes in critical situations; but, as a rule, the Carter administration was less likely to use such tactics. See chapter 2 for additional discussion on this point.

the "deadmen"—those who were leaving Congress—if the latter wanted positions in government. One such member of Congress was Ted Risenhoover (D-OK), who had been defeated in the Democratic primary. Moore wrote to Carter that Risenhoover is "one of those who will not be returning to the House in January. He is looking for a 'future in government.' You should indicate to him that a vote for us on this bill will be remembered."[11] Carter made a note for Bill Cable to "see" Risenhoover the next morning, making a note to move him from "undecided" to "leaning yes."[12] Analysis of those members who were leaving Congress at the end of the session shows that twenty-eight of the fifty-eight switched in order to support Carter, whereas only seven of the fifty-eight switched in order to support Bevill. While we cannot know for sure why these members changed their votes, the Burton-Moore "deadmen" strategy has some explanatory power in this instance.

Carter made a special appeal to some of the members of the Georgia delegation. Doug Barnard (D) was noted by Herky Harris as the "key" member of this delegation. But Harris told the president that Barnard was "in a bind because of Russell Dam. He had help from Tom Bevill and others in restoring funding for it last year. Doug feels some sense of loyalty to them and neglected by us."[13]

A common theme that repeatedly came up in Carter's discussions with members of Congress was the idea of congressional unity. Members' personal and committee positions often commit them to supporting their colleagues and the institution regard-

---

[11] Memorandum to the president from Frank Moore, "To Ask Their Support of the Public Works Veto," October 4, 1978, Jimmy Carter Library, Personal Secretary Handwriting File, Box 105, 10/5/78.

[12] Ibid.

[13] Memorandum for the president from Hubert Harris, "Public Works Veto," October 4, 1978, Jimmy Carter Library, Office of Congressional Liaison, Box 45, Public Works Appropriations [1].

less of presidential influence. Resistance to presidential influence over the appropriations process, which Congress jealously guards—and water projects in particular—was a source of rhetorical leverage for Bevill and his colleagues who supported the appropriations bill and the subsequent veto-override attempt. In meeting with members of Congress, Bevill often highlighted the threat of the executive branch dictating appropriations decisions. In a "Dear Colleague" letter the day before the House vote on the appropriations bill, Majority and Minority Leaders Jim Wright and John Rhodes (AZ), respectively, along with Subcommittee Chair Tom Bevill and Ranking Member John Myers (IN), wrote to their colleagues in opposition to an amendment, consistent with the president's position, for full funding of water projects:

> The Committee...opposes this amendment, for monitoring project scope, progress and public interest, and would leave the allocation and use of project funds entirely to the discretion of the Administration. The Committee believes that the annual review and appropriations are just as essential for effective oversight of water and power development projects as they are for other Federal programs. The Committee has worked very hard to complete its analysis and to report its bill on a schedule to meet the requirements of the Congressional Budget Act, and, thereby, to protect the prerogatives of the Congress in a responsible way.[14]

In a meeting with members and supporters of the appropriations bill, Bevill reinforced the general position that presidential influence over water projects would neuter Congress' power to appropriate, and he threatened members' congressional powers.

---

[14] "To Our Colleagues in Congress," from Jim Wright, John Rhodes, Tom Bevill, and John Myers, June 13, 1978, *Tom Bevill Congressional Papers*, Box 6572, Folder 8.

He argued that excessive administration influence would mean that the "President will write future appropriations bills and the Congress will be relinquishing its constitutional responsibility in the matter of providing future appropriations." Further, he added, "If they have their way, then there will be no use for you to write the Committee or appear before the Committee for projects. OMB will have the final say as to which projects are added, not the Congress."[15] From Bevill's view, the threat was clear: the executive branch was seeking to expand its power in a way that would rob Congress of its constitutional powers. This must have been a particularly effective appeal on two levels: first, in a post-Watergate Congress that was pushing back against presidential power, members were especially suspicious of executive encroachments; and second, surrendering power to the executive and OMB would rob members of their ability to use their personal skills and power to determine funding for projects in their districts that presumably carried with them political benefits. On this view, the president and OMB might well be able to manipulate elections by choosing winners and losers in the fight for project funding. This view was echoed by other members. A Dear Colleague letter, written by several members of the New York delegation, argued the following:

> [T]he White House is challenging the very heart of the Congressional process. President Carter is attempting to force what amounts to a line-item veto on the House by demanding that only a bill which carries projects anointed by the White House will be accepted.[16]

---

[15] "Agenda: Meeting with Interested Members Public Works Appropriations FY '79 Bill," *Tom Bevill Congressional Papers*, Box 6572, Folder 8.
[16] "To Members of the New York State Delegation," from Stanley Lundine, Jack Kemp, Benjamin Gilman, and Henry Nowak, June 14, 1978, *Tom Bevill*

If these arguments were not enough, simple peer pressure and threats of reciprocity were repeated through the halls of Congress. Herky Harris warned that Jack Brinkley (D-GA) "is under much peer pressure to vote to override."[17] And Billy Evans (D-GA) "is on Public Works…[and is under tremendous peer pressure] to support the veto override."[18] Allen Ertel (D-PA), also a member of Public Works, was described as having "received advance pressure from his colleagues to vote to override."[19] A member of Carter's administration called Claude Pepper to urge him to vote to sustain the veto. Pepper said that "there is sort of a fraternity here in that if he votes against someone else's project which might be contained in the overall bill, then they would vote against his…and it's one of those times to help one another."[20] Pepper said he wished the president would realize how little money was truly at stake.

Every encounter with a member became an opportunity for the president to lobby members: Representative Dan Rostenkowski (D-IL) wanted to bring his three daughters to the White House to have their picture taken with the president; the daughters had been in town for a party hosted by the president's son (Chip). Frank Moore advised the president: "If you have the opportunity walking over to the Family Dining Room, I suggest that you ask Dan to help in sustaining the anticipated veto of the Public Works Appropriations Bill." In a follow-up phone call a week later, the president asked Rostenkowski to work on a number of members

---

Congressional Papers, Box 6572, Folder 8.

[17] Memorandum for the president from Hubert Harris, October 4, 1978, "Public Works Veto," Jimmy Carter Library, Office of Congressional Liaison, Box 45, Public Works Appropriations [1].

[18] Ibid.

[19] Ibid.

[20] Ibid.

in the Illinois delegation for their votes. Personally, Rostenkowski promised what help he could give, though on the final vote he voted for the override, likely out of deference for Jim Wright, for whom he had whipped votes in the majority leader's race a year earlier.

Carter enlisted the help of other members of Congress, including Phil Burton, the mercurial Democrat who had lost the job of majority leader by a single vote to Jim Wright. Burton perhaps had in mind a future challenge to Wright, who was on the other side of the veto vote. In the talking points for the meeting, drafted by the congressional liaison, Frank Moore, Carter was advised: "He should be thanked for his invaluable support on the carrier veto override which he viewed as a major effort on his part and *an indirect confrontation with Jim Wright.*" Moore continued, "*He is planning to escalate his opposition to Wright using the Public Works Bill as a vehicle* and it is our judgment that he plans to carry on his attack against Wright using the energy bill as a final victory."[21] Moore had identified a fissure within the House Democrats and sought to take advantage of that in order to help the president. While it is impossible to know with certainty exactly whom Burton whipped on behalf of the president, analysis of the California delegation suggests that he might have had some influence. While the president personally contacted only one member of the delegation, fourteen of the eighteen delegation members who switched their votes on the veto override switched to support Carter; that may indicate the influence of Burton.[22]

---

[21] Memo to the president from Frank Moore, "Meeting with Rep. Phil Burton," September 26, 1978, Jimmy Carter Library, Personal Secretary Handwriting File, Box 103, 9/27/78 [1]; emphasis added.

[22] Eleven of the fourteen who switched votes were Democrats, and it would be among the California Democrats where Burton might have had the most influence.

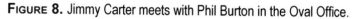

FIGURE 8. Jimmy Carter meets with Phil Burton in the Oval Office.

Source. Courtesy of the Jimmy Carter Library and Museum.
Note. In a White House meeting with President Carter, Representative Phil Burton (D-CA) expressed his support for a veto of the Energy and Water Appropriations Bill. Burton would later work with the president to whip up enough votes to sustain the veto in the House. Burton may have had plans to use the veto override vote to overthrow Majority Leader Jim Wright.

One of the resources that Carter's congressional foes had working for them that the president did not have was the ability to influence projects in members' districts, that is, the ability to threaten those projects. Fred Richmond (D-NY) was just such a member. Moore noted the following:

> Richmond was with us and switched to a "No" after very heavy pressure from Wright and others. Apparently, he has been told that if he and other New Yorkers vote to sustain, it will mean that key urban initiatives will be jettisoned in retaliation. You should reassure Richmond that

we will fight just as hard <u>FOR</u> our key urban programs as we have other key issues, including this one.

Carter noted the following: "Feels very bad—wants Wright to work out a deal." Carter's marginal note indicated that Richmond's vote could not be counted on, and that he would probably support the override.[23] Several other members suggested that they had been told that a vote to sustain the veto would lead to negative consequences.

While we do not know who all of these members were, we do know that Tom Bevill had noted among his contacts several who had projects that might be threatened by a veto. Among those whom Bevill contacted where there was no project at stake, almost 60% converted to the *president's* position, even though they were not contacted directly by the president. Similarly, among those whom Bevill contacted—and the president did not—who had projects at stake, 60% switched to the president's position. Finally, four members with projects were contacted by both Carter and Bevill, and they split these members equally. In short, on this issue, Frank Moore's concern that the president had no chance going up against a powerful member of the Appropriations Committee seems to be overstated; Carter fought Bevill and won.

PRESIDENTIAL INFLUENCE IN CONGRESS: A SUMMARY

Is the president able to influence votes in Congress? Was President Carter able to influence members to help sustain his veto? Measuring the influence of a president centers on his ability to

---

[23] Memorandum for the president from Hubert Harris, October 4, 1978, "Public Works Veto," Jimmy Carter Library, Office of Congressional Liaison, Box 45, Public Works Appropriations [1]; emphasis (underline) original.

influence members "at the margins"—influence is not about a president's ability to influence large numbers of members, but to influence the number of members necessary to be victorious on a given vote. In considering President Carter's abilities as a legislative leader in this case, it is about him being able to influence 30–50 members of Congress to shift from positions of nonsupport to a vote sustaining his veto. The most direct way to examine the influence of the president, and his opponents, is to consider the behavior of members who were contacted and asked to support their positions. According to White House records, the president contacted sixty-seven members of Congress: were those who were contacted by the president more likely to change their position, to switch from a position that did not support the president's policy agenda to a vote supporting the president? Were those eighty-five members contacted by Representative Bevill likely to support his position of overriding the president's veto? Were they more likely when they had a project in the bill, noted by Bevill, and which might have been at risk if the veto was sustained?

Table 6 affords some insight into these questions. Member behavior is grouped into four categories. Two of the four categories reflect members who did not change their position. Members who maintained their position either (1) voted with the Edgar Amendment and subsequently voted to sustain the president's veto ("stayed with Carter's position"), or (2) voted against the Edgar Amendment and voted to override the president's veto ("stayed with Bevill's position"). Members who changed their positions either (1) switched from a nonvoting or "no" vote on the Edgar Amendment to a vote sustaining the president's veto ("switched to Carter's position"), or (2) switched from nonvoting or a "yes" vote on the Edgar Amendment to a "yes" on the veto-override vote ("switched to Bevill's position"). The two

Table 6. Direct lobbying of members and influence on the override vote.

	Member Contacted by the following:						
	Neither	Carter, Not Bevill	Bevill No Project	Bevill with project, Not Carter	Both: Bevill with Project	Both: No Project	Row Totals
Switched to Bevill's Position	37 (13.0)	6 (12.2)	—	3 (20.0)	2 (40.0)	1 (9.1)	49
Stayed with Bevill's Position	139 (48.9)	19 (38.8)	12 (24.5)	2 (13.3)	1 (20.0)	1 (9.1)	174
Switched to Carter's Position	65 (22.9)	23 (46.9)	29 (59.2)	9 (60.0)	2 (40.0)	7 (63.6)	135
Stayed with Carter's Position	43 (15.1)	1 (2.0)	8 (16.3)	1 (6.7)	—	2 (18.2)	55
	284	49	49	15	5	11	

Note. Percentages are column percentages.
$\chi^2 = 59.37$ ($p < .000$). $\lambda = .15$ ($p < .001$).

rows that indicate changes in member behavior are shaded gray. Members are classified by their voting behavior and whether they were contacted by the president and/or Tom Bevill in an attempt to influence their vote on the veto override.

Considering the row totals first: 229 members (55% of those voting) maintained their positions on both votes, while 184 members (45%) changed position, indicating a fair amount of position shifting. Of those who shifted, the president was the clear winner, with 135 members (73%) moving to the president's position, and only forty-nine (27%) moving to Bevill's position in favor of the override. The majority of members were not contacted by either man; this is indicative of the limited resources that each man could deploy with regard to personal contact. Both sides also understood that the vote would be won or lost based on the net movement of only a few members, so the focus would be on those most likely to move.

Carter's success with members was good. Among those members whom Carter contacted and Bevill did not, Carter converted twenty-three members, out of forty-nine, to help sustain his veto; twenty-three out of the twenty-nine (79%) who switched their positions switched to support the president. Of the twelve members contacted by both men who switched positions, nine (75%) switched to support the president. These results suggest that the president was successful when lobbying members and is consistent with Frank Moore's general observations about the president's abilities in this regard. According to Moore, "[H]e was very effective, and it's not just hearsay, because you know, I'd see the votes change."[24] Moore added,

---

[24] *Oral History Interview with Frank Moore*, Jimmy Carter Library and Museum, July 30–31, 2002, 53.

[W]e could measure effectiveness very precisely, because we were keeping vote counts, and the next day we'd go see those people [whom Carter had spoken with]...my staff and I would see them in the hall, we'd walk them to the cars, and they'd change; you know, from undecided to for. Or change from against to undecided. So, he moved a lot of votes, a lot of times, on a lot of issues[25]

Table 7 analyzes members who switched support toward or away from the president using congressional subgroups that were used in several earlier tables. Looking at who switched positions helps us to draw some final conclusions about the strategy outlined by the White House. Consistent with White House expectations, members with less seniority were more likely to shift support to the president than to Bevill by large numbers. Also consistent with Moore's strategy, regional differences are apparent in member behavior. Carter's largest gains on the override vote came from the Northeast and Midwest, while Bevill had more success in those areas most likely to be affected by the appropriations bill, the South and West. Marginal members, perhaps presaging rough midterm elections, tilted toward the president and his public posture that the veto was responsible fiscal policy, a good anti-inflationary move. Finally, analysis of members by committee indicates that the president did not make significant inroads into the membership of the Appropriations and Public Works Committees, who hung together on the vote, but did pick up votes from members of Energy and Commerce and Budget as predicted by the veto strategy devised by the Office of Congressional Liaison.

Using a multivariate model to estimate political influence (see appendix for full statistical results), we are able to graphically

[25] Oral History Interview with Frank Moore, Jimmy Carter Library and Museum, July 30–31, 2002, 53.

TABLE 7. Jimmy Carter's and Tom Bevill's specific influences on the House override vote by subgroup.

	Switched to Support Carter	Switched to Support Bevill
Electoral Status		
Frosh	24 (17.8)	8 (16.3)
Class of 1974	34 (25.2)	6 (12.2)
Region		
Northeast	42 (31.1)	10 (20.4)
Midwest	45 (33.3)	9 (18.4)
Border	8 (5.9)	2 (4.1)
South	22 (16.3)	16 (32.7)
West	18 (13.3)	12 (24.7)
Party		
Democrats	93 (68.9)	33 (67.3)
Republicans	42 (31.1)	16 (32.7)
Ideology[a]		
Carter Supporter	49 (37.1)	11 (29.3)
Carter Moderate	43 (32.6)	53 (31.4)
Carter Opponent	40 (30.3)	70 (41.4)
Electoral[b]		
Marginal	26 (20.2)	7 (15.9)
Non-Marginal	103 (79.8)	37 (84.1)
Committees		
Appropriations	8 (5.9)	6 (12.2)
Public Works	8 (5.9)	8 (16.3)
Energy & Commerce	16 (11.9)	1 (2.0)
Budget	7 (5.2)	4 (8.2)

Note. Percentages are in parentheses. They represent the percentage within the whole group who switched to either the president's or Bevill's position.
[a] Ideological categories are based on members' absolute proximity to the president based on Poole and Rosenthal nominate scores. *Supporters* are those within one standard deviation of the president, *moderates* are between one and two standard deviations, and *opponents* are more than two standard deviations from the president. [b] Marginal members received 55% or less of the district vote in the previous election.

represent the coalition-building success on both sides of the water wars (see Figure 9). At the core of the coalition supporting the override were members of the Appropriations and Public Works Committees. Core supporters of the president came from the reformist Watergate babies and from members of the Energy and Commerce Committee. As the water wars progressed, opponents of the president failed to add to their coalition, thus losing votes to the president. Votes to sustain the president's veto benefited from White House coalition-building efforts. Among those most likely to join the president were those members who were directly contacted by the president and those members who were leaving at the end of the session (deadmen). President Carter also won support from members who were contacted by Tom Bevill, suggesting that when a powerful member and the president go head-to-head, the president *can* win. As predicted by Moore, the Northeast–Midwest connection was an important part of the effort to sustain the override.

Figure 10 illustrates the geographic patterns of support for the president in the House. Based on the multivariate statistical model, we calculate the average probability that members from each state will cast a vote in favor of the president's position. The Midwest and the Northeast were most likely to support the president's position. States abutting the lower Mississippi River and in the Alabama region had a low probability of casting supportive votes, as did several of the Rocky Mountain states. The probability of support for the president in the South was generally weak, though it is interesting to note that South Carolina (the home state of Butler Derrick, who was working on the president's behalf) was associated with higher probabilities of support. In short, while the president never publicly cast the conflict as a Frostbelt versus Sunbelt issue—as Tom Bevill complained he did—the likelihood of support for the president

FIGURE 9. Summary of success in coalition building on the veto override vote.

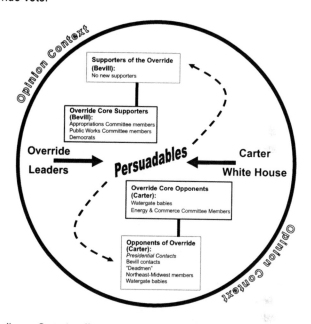

Note. Jimmy Carter's efforts on the veto override motion reaped substantial rewards. Among pursuadables he was able to draw support from a number of groups (*opponents of override*), while Tom Bevill and override supporters (*supporters of override*) saw their support erode in the face of the efforts of Carter and White House efforts.

tended to fall along these geographic divisions, other variables held constant.

The success of the president on the veto override was due, in no small part, to the public relations campaign that was directed out of the White House. Media reaction and public opinion favored the president, as did the activities and opinions of business, taxpayer, and environmental groups in Washington and across the nation. The groundswell of support for the president's position likely translated into negative constituent opinion and more support for sustaining the president's veto than we might have seen otherwise. Some indication of this can be found in Table 6 among those members who were not contacted by the Carter or Bevill; sixty-five of the 102 members who were not contacted by the president or by Bevill voted to sustain the president's veto. It is thus reasonable to conclude that many of these votes were produced by the shift in public opinion that accompanied the public strategy on the vote.

FIGURE 10. Regional distribution of support for Carter on the veto override vote.

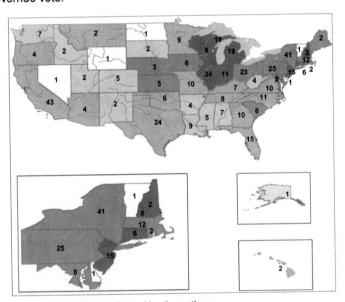

Source. Based on data collected by the authors.
Note. States in the Midwest and the Northeast were the most likely to provide votes to support the president's veto. Darker shading indicates a greater aggregate probability of votes to sustain the veto. States in white are single member states with a probability of zero. Numbers indicate the number of House members from that state.

CHAPTER 5

PRESIDENTIAL INFLUENCE
AND THE POLITICS OF PORK

It was rewarding to prevail even though almost every Democratic leader lined up against me, but the battle left deep scars.

—Jimmy Carter (1995, 84)

In this concluding chapter, we take up several issues. We summarize our findings in light of the existing literature on presidential influence in Congress. Then, we evaluate the veto strategy devised by the Carter White House. Jimmy Carter and his advisers envisioned that his veto would achieve three objectives. Our evaluation centers on the success of the veto strategy for achieving these objectives. Finally, we examine how the Carter veto—this "shot across the bow" of Congress—has influenced the politics of pork over the last thirty years. We contend that the water wars were important for focusing public attention on the pork barrel as a policy concern, as well as for improving the position of future presidents in appropriations politics; Jimmy Carter provided the foundation on which future presidents built their attacks on the congressional pork barrel.

PRESIDENTIAL INFLUENCE IN CONGRESS

The preceding analysis focused on the almost two-year battle between Jimmy Carter and the Democratically controlled Congress over appropriations for water projects. By focusing on a single policy area in which the president was committed to exercise policy and political influence, we focused on a "critical case"—that is, if presidential influence in Congress is not observed in this case, it is unlikely to be observed in those cases in which a president has little policy interest and is unwilling to invest resources in pursuit of policy goals. In short, failure to detect indications of presidential influence in this case suggests that presidential influence is altogether unlikely.

Focusing on this individual case has several benefits. First, we are able to gain additional insight into the contentious relationship between Jimmy Carter and Congress, thereby bringing needed perspective to this topic. Considerable controversy surrounds the legislative leadership abilities of Jimmy Carter. Anecdote, innuendo, ideology, and personal interest have clouded our understanding of Carter as a legislative leader; we bring some analytical perspective to Carter's leadership attributes. More generally, we lift the veil that shrouds the private dealings between presidents and Congress. Our multimethod approach—using archival sources, oral histories, interviews, and biographical resources—places us in unusual proximity to our subjects and allows a greater level of detail regarding attempts at presidential influence than what is usual in political science. Our quantitative analysis benefited substantially from this approach. Our data sources—White House and congressional headcount data, contacts between the president and individual members, and so forth—provide nearly unprecedented information about presidential and congressional attempts to influence individual members of Congress. Using a multimethod approach improves our data. Finally, the multimethod approach we employ here allowed us to test the findings of our analysis by way of the actors and events as they transpired.

Are presidents able to exert influence in Congress to garner support for their legislative priorities and achieve their policy goals? We have marshaled significant evidence to support the proposition that presidents are able to influence the votes of individual members of Congress. The results of our analysis suggest that presidents willing to expend considerable resources are able to influence congressional outcomes. In the case of the Carter administration, this is true despite significant barriers (some of their own making and others that were a matter of circumstance). Using the resources of the White House, presidents attempt to shape the public opinion context. Using a coordinated strategy, implemented over the course of several months, the Carter White House sought to influence media coverage and editorial opinion in favor of the president's position. The White House strategy focused on both the Washington media and the local media in the districts of members believed to be persuadable. They also built coalitions within the Washington community by combining the efforts of interest groups that are often opponents: business, environmental, some labor, and taxpayer groups. By using the power of the presidency to shape the opinion context, the Carter White House created a context in which opposing the president became difficult for many members of Congress. Given the highly salient nature of the veto vote—it was important to Carter for both policy and political reasons—he lobbied dozens of members of Congress directly to garner their support. Victory was hardly ensured in this case. The extraordinary effort by the White House and President Carter to sustain the veto was matched with an impressive effort inside Congress to override the veto. Tom Bevill, Jim Wright, and other members of Congress actively lobbied, cajoled, and perhaps even threatened members to gain their support for the override. That we find support—both qualitative and quantitative—for the influence hypothesis in this hostile political environment makes us all the more confident in our conclusion that presidents are able to exercise influence in Congress.

However, presidents do not exercise influence in Congress equally and at all times. Our results suggest that under some circumstances, a president *may* exercise influence in Congress. When is presidential influence likely to fail? Almost exactly thirty years after Jimmy Carter went to battle with Congress over water projects, President George W. Bush vetoed the Water Resources Development Act of 2007. The events surrounding this veto were, in some ways, oddly similar to Jimmy Carter's veto twenty-nine years earlier.[1] The $23 billion bill passed the House and Senate by veto-proof margins, 381–40 and 81–12, respectively. George Bush argued in his veto message that the bill "lacks fiscal discipline." Bush said that "[t]he House of Representatives took a $15 billion bill into negotiations

---

[1] The Water Resources Development Act of 2007 was an authorizing, rather than an appropriations, bill, and thus is not directly comparable to the bill vetoed by Carter. However, many of the same political dynamics surround the authorization and appropriations of water projects, so a comparison is a useful exercise.

with a $14 billion from the Senate and instead of splitting the difference, emerged with a Washington compromise that costs over $23 billion. This is not fiscally responsible." Unlike Carter, missing from Bush's rhetoric was an appeal to deficits. And, like Carter before him, Bush argued that the "bill does not set priorities." Referring to the need to rationalize water policy, as so many presidents before—including Carter—he said, "My Administration has repeatedly urged Congress to authorize only those projects and programs that provide a high return on invest-ment...American taxpayers should not be asked to support a pork barrel system of Federal authorization and funding where a project's merits is an afterthought."[2]

Congress successfully overrode the Bush veto. Why was Bush unable to sustain his veto? Why did he fail where Jimmy Carter had succeeded? The strategic situation Bush found himself in had changed substantially. During the midterm congressional elections, the Republicans surrendered majorities in the House and Senate to the Democrats, shrinking Bush's core support in Congress. Carter enjoyed a Democratic majority during the water wars. George Bush was solidly established as a lame-duck president, while Jimmy Carter's future in the White House was years from being decided. George Bush's public approval was at a near-historic low with just over 30% job approval; even loyal Republicans did not need to fear presidential retribution. Now in the minority, the Republicans could cast a vote in favor of popular projects in their districts while pointing at the majority Democrats as the party of wastrels. Carter's public approval, while slipping, was considerably higher. Moreover, Hurricane

---

[2] Press release, "President Bush Vetoes Water Resources Development Act of 2007," November 2, 2007, http://www.whitehouse.gov (accessed December 10, 2007).

Katrina had changed public perceptions of water projects in 2005. The hurricane had powerfully illustrated the importance of levies, flood control projects, pumping stations, and critical wetlands. It illustrated how vulnerable Americans could be in the face of the awesome power of nature. The bill would fund reconstruction in the Southeast, but also fund similar—and not so similar—projects in other parts of the country. Without a means for distinguishing worthy from unworthy projects, the public was more sympathetic to pleas on behalf of the bill.

The political feature that had changed most noticeably between 1978 and 2007 was the alignment of interest groups in Washington. During the water wars, Carter was able to unite business and environmental interests against the water projects. The 2007 bill, in contrast, was *supported* by both business and environmental groups that helped to provide support for the override movement. United in supporting the bill were the fiscally conservative and well-funded U.S. Chamber of Commerce and the environmental group, The Nature Conservancy. Environmental groups supported the act due to provisions aimed at preserving and restoring critical water resources and habitats. And labor groups—split during the water wars—were also united in support of the override in 2007. Isolated within the interest group network surrounding this issue in opposition to the bill were the taxpayers groups Taxpayers for Common Sense, the National Taxpayers Union, and Citizens Against Government Waste—all strong allies of the Bush White House.[3]

---

[3] During the debate on the override motion, Senator Barbara Boxer listed the interest groups supporting the veto override (*Congressional Record*, November 8, 2007, S 14116–1411):

- **National business and labor groups:** United States Chamber of Commerce, AFL-CIO, The Teamsters Union, National Construction Alliance,

In the final analysis, a strategically and tactically weak Bush White House was rebuffed easily in both chambers, 361–54 in the House and 79–14 in the Senate. Members of Congress of noticeably different political stripes were joined together in their support of a veto override. United in support of an override were the political "odd couple" of liberal Senator Barbara Boxer (D-CA) and arch-conservative and Bush administration stalwart Senator Jim Inhofe (R-OK), the chair and ranking member of the Senate Energy and Public Works Committee. And the irony of their pairing in the debate was not wasted on either of them, with Boxer noting:

> I think everybody knows that when it comes to the environment, Senator Inhofe and I don't exactly see eye to eye. But when it comes to building the infrastructure of the United States of America, taking care of the needs of our communities, making sure there is flood control, that we can move goods because we need to dredge so

---

United Association of Journeymen and Apprentices of the Plumbing and Pipe Fitting Industry of the United States and Canada, United Brotherhood of Carpenters and Joiners of America.

- **Agricultural groups:** American Farm Bureau Federation, National Corn Growers Association, American Soybean Association, Corn Refiners Association, CropLife America, National Association of Wheat Growers, National Council of Farmer Cooperatives, National Farmers Union, National Grain and Feed Association, National Oilseed Processors Association, The Fertilizer Institute, United Egg Producers.
- **National water and infrastructure groups:** National Waterways Conference, The Waterways Council, Water Resources Coalition, American Electric Power, American Society of Civil Engineers, Associated General Contractors of America, American Association of Port Authorities, American Public Works Association, National Association of Flood and Stormwater Management Agencies.
- **National conservation groups:** The Nature Conservancy, National Audubon Society, National Parks Conservation Society, Ducks Unlimited.

many of our port areas, when it comes to making sure we have recreation areas, and, yes, that we do the kind of environmental restoration that will help us with flood control—for example, restoring the great coastal wetlands of Louisiana—we can and do work together.[4]

Other traditional supporters of the Bush administration were also defectors on the veto override bill, including Senate Republican Whip Trent Lott (MS), who noted on the Senate floor that "I understand why the President vetoed it. He is trying to hold the line on spending. Congratulations. That is good." But, Lott also argued, he would support the veto override because of the following:

It is one of the few areas where we actually do something constructive, where you can see physically something the Federal Government has done. It creates jobs. It provides safety and protection, safe drinking water. It is one of the only bills that I think actually produces a positive result.[5]

This comparative exercise suggests that presidential influence in Congress is context-dependent. Table 8 provides a side-by-side comparison of the two vetoes. It suggests that Carter's success was a function of a political context that favored sustaining the veto and his willingness to throw both the power of his presidency and the White House behind the effort. Bush's veto, by contrast, was defeated by the political context combined with a seeming lack of effort on his part to actively build support in Congress for sustaining his veto.[6]

---

[4] *Congressional Record* (November 7, 2007): S 14049.

[5] *Congressional Record* (November 8, 2007): S 14113–14114.

[6] Future scholars with access to the George W. Bush Papers may be able to determine the degree to which this veto was symbolic.

TABLE 8. Carter and Bush vetoes compared.

	Carter Veto	Bush Veto
Issue Context	Budget Deficits/Inflation	Hurricane Katrina
Public Approval of President	Mildly Weak	Weak
White House Resource Utilization	High	Low
Institutional Control	Democratic Majority-Democratic President	Democratic Majority-Republican President
Editorial Opinion	Pro-Veto	Split
Washington Community		
Business Groups	Pro-Veto	Anti-Veto
Labor Groups	Split	Anti-Veto
Environmental Groups	Pro-Veto	Anti-Veto
Taxpayers Groups	Pro-Veto	Pro-Veto
Outcome	Veto Sustained	Veto Overridden

THE WATER PROJECTS VETO AS STRATEGY

The veto strategy developed by the Carter White House had three objectives. First, it was meant to achieve the president's policy goals with respect to his desire to gain control over congressional spending, reduce the deficit, and reduce inflation. In particular, the president was offended by what he perceived as the Congress' spendthrift habits, and members' willingness to compromise the integrity of the environment on the altar of reelection. President Carter thus sought to bring rationality to the chaos of congressional water policy. Second, a presidential veto—or successful veto threat—was meant to improve President Carter's standing with the public. With public opinion in a steep decline, an exercise aimed at projecting the president's resolve was presumed to be important—at least in the eyes of his top political advisers—for improving his public image. Finally, the strategy was aimed at signaling to Congress the president's intention to actively press his policy agenda and to use his position to achieve his policy goals; a Congress successfully tamed would not only deliver on the immediate goal of modifying water policy, but also become more responsive to presidential influence in the future. In this section, we consider the effect of the president's veto on these three objectives: policy, public opinion, and congressional relations.

Post-Veto Water Policy

Jimmy Carter's demand for changes in the way that water projects were considered by Congress was largely successful. The purpose in challenging Congress and using the veto was to eliminate "wasteful" spending and change the standards by which future water projects would be evaluated. Following the veto, the administration entered into a bargaining phase with the House. In order to provide for necessary appropriations, the Energy and Water appropriations would need to be folded into a continuing resolution that was pending in the Senate. But the leverage afforded the administration by sustaining the veto allowed several important and long-lasting changes in future water policy development. The most important demand of the administration was that appropriations bills should include estimates of the full cost of water projects in order to unmask the long-term cost of water projects. Congressional negotiators agreed that the Subcommittee on Energy and Water Appropriations would hold hearings and include such a mechanism in their FY 1980 Appropriations Bill. In order to ensure that full funding would be included in the 1980 bill, the committee further agreed that they would "report full cost of each new start project in the reports on the 1980 bill and each bill thereafter."[7] In addition, the administration insisted

---

[7] Memorandum to the president from Stuart Eizenstat, "Negotiating Points," Jimmy Carter Library, Office of Congressional Liaison, Box 45, Public Works Appropriations [1].

that new water projects be chosen based on criteria that included the environmental impact of a project. Congress agreed in the future to "use new start selection criteria that [were] used in the 1979 [appropriations] bill pending further refinement of criteria with the Administration."[8] In return for these major concessions, Congress insisted that appropriations for the "hit list" projects be continued. The White House also agreed to "accept new project starts, which on a fully funded basis, fit within a budget cap which may range moderately above the Administration's proposal."[9] President Carter and his team wrung significant concessions out of Congress due to Carter's willingness to carry through on his veto threat, and then to defeat the override attempt after investing considerable personal and organizational resources in the fight. By Frank Moore's reckoning, "That's what we did. We changed the standards on that and won. We said that 'from now on you have to do this.'"[10]

Post-Veto Public Opinion

Changing public opinion regarding the president was considered one of the benefits of the use of the veto. President Carter's job approval rating began slipping early in his term and continued to decline throughout his first year in office. While events outside of the president's control drove the decline, his poor relations with Congress and the perception that he was indecisive added to the slide. Ironically, Carter's willingness to accept Tip O'Neill's compromise on the FY 1978 Energy and Water Appropriations Bill likely added to the perception that he was unwilling to stand

[8] Ibid.

[9] Ibid.

[10] *Interview with Frank Moore (including William Cable, Dan Tate, and Robert Thompson)*, Miller Center for Public Affairs Presidential Oral History Program, September 18–19, 1981, 120.

up to Congress or for his beliefs. Use of the veto was intended to improve his public image and to help achieve policy goals, both fiscal and environmental. The use of the veto to improve a president's image may have unintended consequences. As discussed in chapter 1, the existing research suggests that the presidential veto may lead to a decline in presidential approval.

We examine the effect of the veto on presidential approval using two broad indicators: response from the public based on White House mail and the president's approval ratings over the course of his administration. In a given week, the White House receives thousands of pieces of mail from individuals throughout the country. One of the jobs of the White House mailroom is to record the opinions contained in these letters and report them to the president and his advisers. Public opinion expressed through letters to the president is considered important because it represents "activated opinion," that is, the opinions of those individuals willing to take the time and effort to communicate with the White House. Rather than reflecting the casual opinions of individuals included in surveys, these letters require a level of commitment on the part of the authors that goes beyond casual opinionating. In the case of President Carter, we know that he took them seriously enough to view them on a weekly basis, as indicated by his initialing of the reports.[11] Examining the mail summaries for the week prior to the veto and the week after the veto suggests an interesting pattern. In the week prior to the veto, there were not enough letters to the White House about the pending veto to be included in the official summary. In the week following the veto, the White House received over 700 letters regarding the veto, with 98% of those letters indicat-

---

[11] The mail reports were also sent to all of the president's senior advisers.

ing support for the president's veto of the proposed legislation.[12] This seems to indicate the kind of positive bump in public opinion that the president, or at least his political advisers, had hoped to see. But the positive reaction was short lived; two weeks after the veto, it had dropped from the consciousness of White House correspondents, which seems to indicate the transitory nature of the impact of the veto on opinion.

Of course, the hope of the president's political advisers was that the veto would have a positive impact on public approval of the president's performance in office. Figure 11 illustrates job approval of the president by month throughout his term. The first observation is that his job approval ratings indicate a significant overall downward trend. On average, each additional month resulted in a .76 drop in job approval; if we factor out the "benefit" to Carter's public opinion as a result of the Iranian Hostage Crisis (caused by the rally effect), the decline is 1.25 points per month.[13] A second observation is that there is a surge in public approval that roughly coincides with the president's exercise of the veto of the water bill. Between September and October, the president's job approval increased from 43% to 48%, remaining around 50% into January, and is statistically significant.[14] The decline resumed shortly, apparently unabated by the president's veto and successful defense of his veto in the House. Once we take into account the effect of the "veto bump" (and the rally effect surrounding the Hostage Crisis), the decline in job approval increased slightly from 1.25 to 1.31 percentage

---

[12] Memoranda for the president, "Weekly Mail Report (Per Your Request)" from Hugh Carter," Jimmy Carter Library, Personal Secretary Handwriting File, Box 104, October 1978.

[13] We use a naïve model to predict approval: $\text{APPROVAL} = 63.41 - .76(\text{MONTH}) + e$ – adjusted $R^2 = .57$.

[14] $\text{APPROVAL} = 69.49 - 1.25(\text{MONTH}) + 19.27(\text{HOSTAGES}) + e$ – adjusted $R^2 = .76$.

FIGURE **11.** President Carter's public approval, 1977–1980.

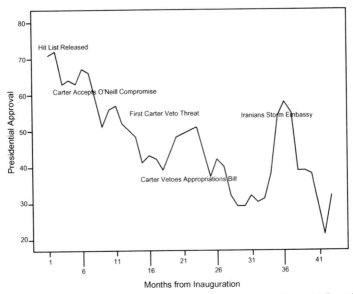

Source. Calculated by the authors from data provided by King and Ragsdale (1988, 292–296).
Note. Public approval of President Carter evidences a general decline throughout his presidency. One notable surge in job approval comes at the same time that the president carried through on his threat to veto the Energy and Water Appropriations Bill. Shortly after the veto, the approval ratings continued their decline.

points per month. These results indicate that in the absence of the veto, the president's approval ratings would have eroded slightly quicker. In short, the veto seems to have had the effect on public opinion that was intended by his political advisers, but the net benefit of the veto was an increase of .06 percentage points per month.[15] Despite the appearance of being at odds with

---

[15] And one more time for the benefit of political scientists: APPROVAL = 69.49 − 1.31(MONTH) + 21.55(HOSTAGES) + 8.29(VETO) + e − adjusted R^2 = .79.

Groseclose and McCarty (2001), there are a number of reasons why our findings are not directly comparable.[16] The bottom line, it seems, is that there was little (if any) public opinion benefit associated with this veto.

Post-Veto Congressional Relations

By all accounts, the Energy and Water veto episode was a bruising battle. One question that remains is whether the battle resulted in improved relations between President Carter and Congress. By simple aggregate statistical measures, it does not seem that the president was more successful in Congress than he was before the veto. During the 95th Congress, northern Democrats voted with the president 74.97% of the time, and in the 96th Congress, they voted with him 75.07% of the time. By comparison, southern Democrats voted with Carter 56.11% of the time during the 95th Congress, and 61.22% of the time in the 96th Congress, a slight improvement.[17] For the most part, Democrats in Congress were supportive of the president, and the president was successful in passing legislation. As Frank Moore said of the president's legislative success:

> I think people confused congressional relations with congressional results...we had a high percentage of the legislation we proposed passed. People remember the fifteen percent we lost rather than the eighty-five percent we passed. I think we had a damn good record of getting our legislation passed.[18]

---

[16] Groseclose and McCarty (2001) examine approval ratings under conditions of divided government only, and they use quarterly aggregations while we look at approval by month. In addition, we employ a simpler model.

[17] Calculated by the authors from King and Ragsdale (1988, 81).

[18] *Interview with Frank Moore (including William Cable, Dan Tate, and Robert Thompson)*, Miller Center for Public Affairs Presidential Oral History Program, September 18–19, 1981, 132.

Looked at in closer detail, the veto had a significant impact on the president's relationships with individual members. Speaking about the president's early challenges to Congress on water projects, Frank Moore said,

> "[I]t did create some bad feelings and we were a long time getting over it, particularly the Public Works Committee and the Appropriations Committee. And I'm not saying it wasn't the right thing to do...I guess what I am saying is that we did it pretty early and there were some unintended consequences."[19]

Among the unintended consequences were bruised feelings among key members of Congress. Shortly after the veto, Senate Democratic Leader Robert Byrd requested a meeting with the president at the White House. In requesting the meeting, Dan Tate related to the president that Robert Byrd wanted to hand deliver a personal letter to Carter, and speculated on Byrd's motive for the meeting:

> [Byrd] manages to mask his outrage with respect to the Public Works Appropriations veto, but if that subject comes up he becomes extremely upset. Since Senator Byrd is such a private person it is difficult to determine exactly the source of his outrage. Based on my conversations with him, I believe he is largely upset because of your "rhetoric." He feels that you have subjected the Congress, which is controlled and led by Democrats, to unnecessary public ridicule and made it especially hard on Democratic Senators who are up for reelection...I have also caught hints of personal embarrassment from

---

[19] *Oral History Interview with Frank Moore*, Jimmy Carter Library and Museum, July 30–31, 2002, 109–110.

him. He alluded to the several times he has gone to Democratic Senators and begged and cajoled them to support their President and had them respond. He says that it will be extremely difficult for him to do that again...There is little doubt that we are on his wrong side now.[20]

Tate concluded the lengthy memo by suggesting that the president should treat Byrd "with a degree of deference." We can only speculate about how Byrd's mood would have been affected by the need to carry the override fight into the Senate, where Byrd would likely have supported the president at the expense of his own support of water projects generally.

If Byrd's mood was an indication of attitudes in the Senate, Bevill's mood could be considered a reflection of attitudes of many in the House. For several days after the failure of the override, Bevill's staff was tasked with performing an extensive analysis of the fatal vote and classifying voters according to their party leadership positions, seniority, and committee membership. In later years, Bevill would say of Carter's hit list: "Well you know Carter's hit list; I finished every one of those projects—finished them and, you know, Carter is gone."[21] Whether Bevill followed through with any threats he may have made to punish members who voted against him in subsequent appropriations bills awaits further analysis. It is suggestive, however, that the only appropriations material that was included in his personal papers revolved around the FY 1980 Energy and Water Appropriations Bill.

---

[20] Memorandum for the president from Dan Tate, "Senator Robert C. Byrd," October 9, 1978, Jimmy Carter Library, Personal Secretary Handwriting File, Box 106, 10/11/78. Unfortunately, Byrd's letter is restricted and not available to researchers.

[21] Telephone interview with a former member of Mr. Bevill's congressional staff, June 2006.

Immediately following the veto-override vote, there was a sense of foreboding among the congressional liaison staff. Les Francis warned the senior staff: "I am concerned that our back-to-back victories of the Defense and Public Works vetoes may inspire an exaggerated sense of confidence or a renewed resolve to adopt a hard-line, no compromise position on other bills that we find disagreeable."[22] In Francis' opinion, the veto fight had been successful, but he warned against potential negative responses from Congress if the administration sought to exercise more muscle than they had gained in the fight:

> When we first presented our veto strategy in late May or early June, its expressed purpose was two-fold: (1) We wanted to increase our leverage on bills that were particularly troublesome...and (2) we wanted to correct the impression on the Hill that Congress could, without thinking twice, force the president to accept almost anything they sent down here. I am firmly convinced that our strategy has been successful on both counts...sustaining the vetoes on defense and public works has convinced many members of Congress that the president is (a) serious about his vetoes and (b) fully capable of making his vetoes stick. Our strategy was sound and effective and should not be abandoned. Neither. However, should we overplay our hand or rub Congress' collective nose in it. To accelerate our strategy at this point would...turn congressional disappointment into bitterness, and bitterness into a determination to "teach us a lesson."

---

[22] Memorandum to Frank Moore from Les Francis, "Revised 'Veto Strategy,'" October 9, 1978, Jimmy Carter Library, Personal Secretary Handwriting File, Box 106, folder 10/11/78.

Carter personally indicated his agreement with Francis' analysis, noting, "I agree."[23] It was a wiser liaison staff that emerged from the fight.

For Frank Moore, Jimmy Carter's relationship with Congress was bound to be rocky. He wrote:

> Even if Jimmy Carter had been elected to three terms, relations were never going to be good with Congress. He was an activist president, and most congressmen don't want to vote on something controversial. He was pushing tough, hard legislation, things that had been left behind for years. Things that a guy knew that if he voted on it he was going to make fifty-one percent of the people in his district mad at him, or forty-nine percent, or forty percent. They'd rather not vote on it at all. The way to have good congressional relations is not to send any controversial legislation to the Hill."[24]

Moore concluded on a sarcastic note:

> [W]e could have had a great congressional liaison if all we wanted to do was take people on the Sequoia and ride them up and down on the Potomac, or go to the Kennedy Center, or just go to fund-raisers. You can get good congressional relations, but you don't get any legislation passed.[25]

---

[23] Ibid.

[24] *Interview with Frank Moore (including William Cable, Dan Tate, and Robert Thompson)*, Miller Center for Public Affairs Presidential Oral History Program, September 18–19, 1981, 132.

[25] Ibid.

THE WATER WARS AND THE POLITICS OF PORK

The 2005 transportation bill included $223 million for a bridge—actually a twin-span bridge—from the Alaska mainland across a quarter-mile wide Tongass Narrows from Gravina Island to Revillagigedo Island, home to 13,000 Alaskans. Senator Ted Stevens (R-AK) and Representative Don Young (R-AK) were the chief congressional proponents of the project. For residents of the island, the project would be a welcome alternative to using a ferry or water taxi to get to their homes in Ketchikan from the Ketchikan Airport. Stevens and Young argued that the bridge would promote development on the island by making it more accessible. Opponents of the project dubbed the project the "bridge to nowhere." The bridge project became the latest poster child for "wasteful government spending." President Bush cited the overall cost of the bill as the basis of his threat to veto the legislation. House Majority Leader Tom Delay (R-TX) argued to his Republican colleagues that their party was in danger of losing its reputation as the party of fiscal responsibility by funding this and other pork barrel projects. He suggested that the Republican majority trim the spending in the bill and begin by eliminating the bridge project. Senator Stevens heatedly objected to Delay's suggestion that the project be removed from the bill, and he went so far as to threaten to quit the Senate if his project was not funded. Ultimately, a compromise was reached that met with the Bush administration's approval while retaining funding for Alaska.[26]

The battle over the bridge to nowhere is, in some respects, a child of the water wars. At the outset of the water wars, the

---

[26] In the final bill, Alaska was granted the funds but without the condition that the funds be used for the proposed bridge project.

congressional pork barrel was largely obscured from public view. The progressive reforms that opened Congress in the 1970s helped to shed some light on congressional process, but educating the media and informing the public remained a significant challenge:

> We tried but it was really tough to make a poster child, a 'bridge to nowhere,' in those days. It was a different era of media coverage...During the water fight it was very difficult to interest the media in the details of these projects.[27]

The water wars created a strategic and rhetorical roadmap that was employed by Ronald Reagan and successive presidents in their attempts to challenge Congress' power of the purse. In fact, during the 1980 presidential campaign and throughout his presidency, Ronald Reagan intensified Carter's initial attack on the congressional pork barrel, arguing that a balanced budget could be achieved by eliminating "waste, fraud, and abuse" in federal spending.

But it was not until near the end of the Reagan presidency that those White House efforts to infiltrate the congressional pork barrel took a rhetorical quantum leap. In his final State of the Union address, Reagan sought to reframe pork by focusing on individual examples of "wasteful" congressional appropriations. Referring to the omnibus appropriations bill the Congress sent to the White House some weeks earlier, Reagan pointed out to the American public that

> there's millions for items such as cranberry research, blueberry research, the study of crawfish, and the commer-

---

[27] Dale Leibach, interview with the authors, August 10, 2007, Washington, DC.

cialization of wild flowers. And that's not to mention the $5 million [White House correction: $.5 million] or so—that—so that people from developing nations could come here to watch Congress at work."[28]

This characterization cast congressional expenditures in a new light by focusing attention on small expenditures of apparently dubious value to illustrate why the executive branch should be granted more control over congressional spending. In fact, Reagan used these examples to make a plea for a presidential line-item veto that would provide the president with the ability to veto specific appropriations. Small examples like these provided the public with a new way to understand congressional pork.

The most enduring example of this new approach to exposing congressional pork came in 1990, when the nation's attention was focused on an (arguably) especially egregious example of a pork barrel expenditure: the Lawrence Welk Museum. During 1990, the Democratic Congress and the George H. W. Bush administration engaged in a pitched battle over the FY 1991 budget. That battle resulted in President Bush breaking his "no new taxes pledge." In the appropriations process, Senator Quentin Burdick (D-ND) worked to include $500,000 of funding for a German-Russian Interpretive Center, using the house and the grounds of Mr. Welk's childhood home in Strasburg, North Dakota. The Bush White House attacked the project as an example of all that was wrong with the congressional appropriations process. At a campaign stop in San Francisco, Bush criticized Congress:

> At the same time this President and these Republican members were doing our level-best to curtail spending, Congress

---

28 Ronald Reagan, State of the Union Address, 1988.

voted to spend a half a million dollars to create a Lawrence Weld tourist attraction. And we all like Lawrence Welk, 'dah-dee-dah', you know how he is. But I cite this as a symptom of the problem. (quoted in Dowd 1990, A1)

Using the Lawrence Welk Museum as exhibit number one, they successfully shifted the issue frame to an episodic frame (see chapter 4); by focusing attention on a single example, they were able to create a useful frame for public understanding. The Bush White House was the first to successfully create a poster child example of the congressional pork barrel.

Successive presidents have used the same approach when attacking congressional expenditures; the success of the "bridge to nowhere" as a symbol of congressional misappropriation is the result of this shift in the issue frame. President Clinton was careful not to embarrass Congress when he had the short-lived power of line-item veto by not singling out specific projects for ridicule. However, during his last year in office, Clinton rescinded $478 million from 2,372 congressional earmarks, and the administration did highlight one project in particular—the LHD-8, a $1.5 billion helicopter carrier that was not requested by the Navy, but which was scheduled to be built in Mississippi, home of Senate Majority Leader Trent Lott (Pear 2000). Not to be outdone by his father, however, George W. Bush ramped up the public education effort by attempting to further lay bare the congressional appropriations process in a way that would buttress support for increased executive power. In his 2007 State of the Union address, Bush—for the first time of which we are aware—used the inside-the-beltway term "earmark" to place a name on the congressional practice of directing spending to their districts:

Next, there is the matter of earmarks. These special interest items are often slipped into bills at the last hour—when not even C-SPAN is watching. In 2005 alone, the number of earmarks grew to over 13,000 and totaled nearly $18 billion. Even worse, over 90 percent of earmarks never make it to the floor of the House and Senate—they are dropped into committee reports that are not even part of the bill that arrives on my desk. You didn't vote them into law. I didn't sign them into law. Yet, they're treated as if they have the force of law. The time has come to end this practice. So let us work together to reform the budget process, expose every earmark to the light of day and to a vote in Congress, and cut the number and cost of earmarks at least in half by the end of this session.

For the first time, earmarks entered into the public vocabulary and, with the Democrats in control of the Congress, "earmark reform" assumed a central role in the early agenda of the new majority, resulting in new rules that were presumed to lower pork production.[29]

• • •

The Founding Founders created an arena of potentially significant conflict between Congress and the executive branch by providing for the executive veto. Since the beginning of the twentieth century, presidents have sought to employ the veto power as a mechanism of influence, threatening or using the veto to pressure Congress to adopt legislation more to the liking of the president. More recently, presidents have sought aggressively to assert influence over Congress' constitutionally mandated "power

---

[29] Subcommittees of the full Appropriations Committee were instructed to detail specific earmarks contained in their bills in their committee reports. Some subcommittees took the opportunity to highlight "presidential pork," location-specific projects for which funding was requested (earmarks) by the White House.

of the purse." Charging Congress with irresponsible spending habits, Nixon impounded funds; Carter used the veto; Reagan, Bush, and Clinton used the veto and sought line-item veto power; and George W. Bush returned to the veto. The terrain where the veto power meets the pork barrel provides a vantage point from which to observe how presidents seek to influence individual members of Congress and influence Congress' constitutional power to spend money. By taking advantage of this confluence of institutional interests and powers, we addressed whether presidents are able to exercise influence in Congress and how Congress seeks to push back against attempts at influence when they intersect with its most jealously guarded prerogative. Conflict arising from Constitutional design, namely, the competition for superiority—the conquest of one set of institutional interests over another—is as predictable as the Constitution is eternal. How each battle is decided depends on the politics of the day and the abilities of the combatants—that is, the ability of a president and members of Congress to shape the politics of the day and build winning coalitions.

THE PORK BARREL
AND BEYOND

I first met Scott Frisch and Sean Kelly at the Carter Conference in Athens, Georgia, in January 2007. The first thing I said to them was that I didn't think anyone would ever get this story right. In this book, they "get it right." Academicians will no longer point to the fight over the water projects as an example of the "incompetence" or "ineffectiveness" of President Carter and his advisers. As the authors show, President Carter was able to change minds in Congress and produce substantive changes in policy. In fact, if I may say, we did really well in passing the Carter agenda. Carter's record in passing his legislative agenda compares favorably to the records of other modern presidents.[1]

With regard to the battle with Congress over the water projects, were some mistakes made? Sure. We broke some dishes and perhaps handled the rollout of the "hit list" with less finesse than we might have. It may even be fair to say that some of the damage caused by the fight against the water projects was not repairable. But Jimmy Carter was interested first and foremost in what was best for the country. He approached these projects with concerns about the budget, wasteful spending, and the concerns of a true environmentalist. President Carter became the first president in modern times to apply specific criteria and rational decision making to the earmark process.

Jimmy Carter made these tough decisions, and it was hell to pay in the districts of some members whose projects were cut. Among affected constituents were my parents! One of the threatened projects, the Columbia Tennessee Dam, was in my hometown. Folks all around town knew that I worked for Jimmy Carter, and my parents often received quite an earful. Every spring, the city fathers of Columbia came to Washington to make the case for the dam: It would provide the water needed for economic development. The veto infuriated the city fathers, and Carter got all the blame. The dam was ultimately done in by Ronald Reagan for budgetary reasons. Then, Columbia got the biggest auto manufacturing plant in the world: the GM Saturn plant. Carter was right—they didn't need the dam.

Drawing on my observations over the last thirty years, I'd like to reflect on the culture of pork barrel politics that has developed

---

[1] According to the *Congressional Quarterly Almanac* (1980, 17C-23C), President Carter's congressional support scores averaged about 75% during his four-year term.

in Washington since the battles over the water projects. I offer some advice to coming administrations and the Congress about how to gain control over the problem of earmarks. If there is any one lesson of the last thirty years that stands out to me, it is the belief that most of federal spending should be determined by Congress. But the president, Congress, and the media all have roles to play.

THE CURRENT PROBLEM

Occasionally, I tell people that the biggest war in Washington is not the Iraq War, it is earmarks. Carter's fight against the water projects was the first effort to rein in earmarks. President Carter's efforts, and especially the veto, were a cannon blast across the bow of Congress on pork.

Over the last decade, things have gone from bad to worse. A recent report from the Congressional Research Service simply reinforces the fact (CRS 2006). Take, for instance, the growth in earmarks in the Labor-HHS Appropriations Bill. In 1994 there were five earmarks in the bill. By the year 2000, there were almost 500 earmarks, and by 2005 more than 3,000 earmarks! Even the number of earmarks in the Energy and Water Appropriations Bill, which has typically been very high, has increased by about 50% between 1994 and 2005. The report shows that earmark growth skyrocketed during the six years of Republican control of the White House and Congress. Now, it is true that most earmarks still come from the executive branch. Most of the decisions about discretionary spending come from the White House, and that's pork too.

Based on my observations on the politics of pork, I have come to the conclusion that most of the decisions about projects still need to be made in Congress. The power of the purse belongs to Congress. What is important is that these decisions be made with transparency. As a senior member of Congress recently told me, it seems that casework, which used to be the bread and butter of a congressional office, has been replaced with earmarks and fund raising. Earmarks have become a specialty for some lobby firms, much like the tax industry.

It wasn't until outright abuses surfaced—as in the case of Duke Cunningham, a Republican from California—that anyone took much notice of the abuse of earmarks. Unfortunately, it takes a scandal to move the meter, to make some progress. With transparency, it may be that the media can become a check on Congress. It might be that the press could do for Congress what it has difficulty doing for itself.

ADVICE FOR THE NEXT ADMINISTRATION AND CONGRESS

The key to changing the politics of the pork barrel spending and restoring fiscal sanity is to increase transparency. Since taking control of Congress in 2007, the House Democratic leadership has made some strong steps in this direction. The next president must use the bully pulpit of the presidency to shine a light, to make the public pay attention to earmarking.

The next president must be willing to challenge Congress on spending issues as Jimmy Carter did. It is not easy, but it is a reflection of the job that the Founding Fathers invested in the president when they wrote the U.S. Constitution.

The presidency is the office in our system that specifically has the institutional role to watch out for the national interest. But the president must be willing to work with Congress to find a solution. When is an earmark an "earmark" or "pork," and when is it a federally funded project that benefits constituents? Certainly, money for a college research lab might be appropriate, or money for advanced science and most infrastructure, but a road project 8,000 miles from a member's constituents probably is not.

Finally, in order for this to work, the media needs to pay attention to earmarking. Press oversight can provide a check on earmarks if they are willing to invest resources into serious journalism. They have to commit to covering the details of governing and ignore the foibles of celebrities. With pressure to focus on the financial bottom line, the media seems all too willing to focus on what sells, and not what is important. The media needs to return to its role as the protector of the public interest. And it is in the public interest to get control of pork barrel spending.

Jim Free
Former Special Assistant to President Carter
for Congressional Relations

APPENDIX

FULL MODEL
OF PRESIDENTIAL INFLUENCE
ON THE VETO OVERRIDE

In this short appendix, we discuss a multivariate model that seeks to estimate the impact of presidential influence on votes to sustain the president's veto. For the nontechnical reader, the purpose of this estimation technique (logistic regression) is aimed at providing a rigorous test of one of the major hypotheses of this book, that is, that President Carter was able to exercise personal influence to change the minds of some members of Congress and sustain his veto. This statistical approach allows us to rule out alternative causes for the patterns—which seem to indicate that the president was successful in his lobbying efforts—that we have identified throughout the book, thus increasing our confidence in our findings.

Table A-1 provides results for two models. One includes measures used throughout the paper (model one) and the other maintains only those variables (save one) that are consistently shown to have some value for predicting how members of Congress would vote on the veto override (model two). Our primary interest is in those variables that attempt to get at the concept of influence. One of these variables is the presidential contact variable. Our results indicate that, other factors being held constant, contact with president Carter made members of Congress more likely to cast a vote to support his veto; in fact, the results indicate that the president's efforts doubled

TABLE A-1. A multivariate model of presidential influence on the veto override vote in the House.

	Switched Vote to Support Carter = 1 (Model One)	e^b	Switched Vote to Support Carter = 1 (Model Two)	e^b
Political Influence				
Presidential Contact = 1	.75** (5.51)	2.11	.77*** (5.99)	2.17
Deadmen = 1	.63* (3.33)	1.89	.71** (4.54)	2.04
Bevill Contact = 1	1.23*** (15.98)	3.43	1.25*** (16.81)	3.49
Ideology				
Veto Pivot = 1	084 (.09)	—	.02 (.004)	—
Region				
Northeast = 1	.76*** (5.63)	2.15	.77*** (6.06)	2.15
Midwest = 1	1.02*** (9.86)	2.78	1.03*** (10.13)	2.81
Electoral Status				
Sophomore = 1	.71** (4.76)	2.03	.72** (4.93)	2.05
Marginal = 1	.22 (.38)	—	—	—
Committees				
Appropriations = 1	-1.16*** (6.57)	.31	-1.27*** (8.28)	.31
Public Works = 1	-1.10** (5.25)	.33	-1.19** (6.33)	.33
Energy & Commerce = 1	.16 (.15)	—		
Budget = 1	.25 (.22)	—		
Constant	-1.38 (.22)		-1.30 (35.26)	
Model Fit				
Pseudo-R^2	.26		.26	
$-2 \times$ LLR	380.49		390.16	
Correctly Predicted	68.2%		69.8%	

Note. The dependent variable is coded 1 if the member switched to support the president's position and 0 if the member stayed with or switched to support Bevill's position. "Deadmen" is coded 1 if the member was leaving the institution as the close of the Congress (see text for more discussion of this concept). Numbers in parentheses are t-wald. e^b is reported only if the coefficient is significant at the .05 level or below.
*p < .05. **p < .01. ***p < .001. (one-tailed probabilities)

the likelihood of a "no" vote. The results also support that the "Burton strategy" of appealing to members who were leaving Congress had an impact. Our operationalization of this concept is admittedly crude; we included as "deadmen" those members who were leaving the institution not those who were given indications by the White House that their loyalty would be repaid (there is no archival record to establish what promises may or may not have been made).[1] Deadmen were twice as likely to vote with the president. Finally, contact with Chairman Bevill seems to have had the opposite effect of that which he might have intended. In the presence of pressure being applied by both sides, Bevill was losing votes despite his efforts at contacting members. These results hold across both models.

Support for Krehbiel's (1998) conception of voting behavior as a function of policy preferences is not supported in these findings. It does not appear that members to the political left of the veto pivot were more likely to vote with the president than are those to the right of the pivot. We left the variable in the second model nonetheless, where it fails to perform as predicted.

Our results suggest that there was a strong regional component to the veto-override vote. Members from the Northeast and Midwest were highly likely to switch positions to support the president, reflecting the idea that Frank Moore's strategy of targeting members from these two regions was wise indeed; northern members were twice as likely to support the president, and Midwestern members were almost three times as likely to support the president. It appears that the president and his advisers were able to successfully cast the battle as one between the Sunbelt and the Frostbelt. As Bevill observed at the time, a major

---

[1] That there is no record is not surprising. It reflects the old political maxim: "Why write it down if you can *say it*, and why say it if a *nod* will do?"

theme of the White House "was that the South and West have been getting far more water projects than the East. Somehow [they] did not get around to explaining the reasons why this is so: There is more water to utilize in the South and there is a greater need for water storage in the West" (Free 1978, 6).

The electoral variables included in the model tell two stories. First, marginal members were not more likely than non-marginal members to support the president's position. This indicates that the White House's public strategy was not resulting in enough pressure on these more vulnerable members that they felt they had to side with the president. It is the case, however, that sophomore members (the Watergate babies) were significantly more likely to support the president on the veto vote; sophomore members were twice as likely to switch to support the president as either first-term or more senior members. This may reflect the shared reform ethos that swept the sophomores and the president into office. The lack of support from first-term members in particular would seem to endorse the idea that they did not feel that they owed their jobs to the president.

Finally, committee position does matter. Members of the Appropriations Committee and Public Works were steadfast against switching; membership on either committee reduced the likelihood of a switch by more than 70%. This indicates that either shared interests or committee pressure united these members and kept them from shifting to the president's position.

One of the benefits of this multivariate statistical approach is that it can be used to calculate individual probabilities that each member would switch to support the president. These individual probabilities were aggregated to the state level and used in this book (see Figure 9).

REFERENCES

Bonafede, Dom. 1977. Carter and Congress: It Seems That if Something Can Go Wrong, It Will. *National Journal* (November 12): 1756.

Bond, Jon R., and Richard Fleisher. 1994. Carter and Congress: Presidential Style, Party Politics, and Legislative Success. In *The Presidency and Domestic Policies of Jimmy Carter*, ed. Herbert D. Rosenbaum and Alexej Ugrinsky, 287–298. Westport, CT: Greenwood Press.

Brown, Lawrence D., James W. Fossett, and Kenneth T. Palmer. 1984. *The Changing Politics of Federal Grants*. Washington, DC: The Brookings Institution.

Browne, William P. 1998. *Groups, Interests, and U.S. Public Policy*. Washington, DC: Georgetown University Press.

Bumiller, Elisabeth. 2002. Memo Shows White House Ire on Budget Criticism. *New York Times*, March 8.

Cameron, Charles M. 2000. *Veto Bargaining: Presidents and the Politics of Negative Power*. New York: Cambridge University Press.

Cameron, Charles M., John S. Lapinski, and Charles R. Reimann. 2000. Testing Formal Theories of Political Rhetoric. *Journal of Politics* 62: 187–205.

Carter, Jimmy. 1995. *Keeping Faith: Memoirs of a President*. Fayetteville: University of Arkansas Press.

Clymer, Adam. 1977. Carter's Opposition to Water Projects Linked to '73 Veto of Georgia Dam. *New York Times*, June 13, p. 14.

————. 2008. *Drawing the Line at the Big Ditch: The Panama Canal Treaties and the Rise of the Right.* Lawrence: University of Kansas Press.

Congressional Research Service (CRS). 2006. Earmarks in Appropriation Acts: FY 1994, FY 1996, FY 1998, FY 2000, FY 2002, FY 2004, FY 2005, January 26.

Conley, Richard S., and Amie Kreppel. 2001. Toward a New Typology of Vetoes and Overrides. *Political Research Quarterly* 54: 831–852.

Copeland, Gary W. 1983. When Congress and the President Collide: Why Presidents Veto Legislation. *Journal of Politics* 45: 696–710.

Davis, Eric L. 1979. Legislative Liaison in the Carter Administration. *Political Science Quarterly* 95: 287–302.

————. 1983. Congressional Liaison: The People and the Institutions. In *Both Ends of the Avenue: The Presidency, the Executive Branch, and Congress in the 1980s*, ed. Anthony King, 59–95. Washington, DC: American Enterprise Institute.

Deen, Rebecca E., and Laura W. Arnold. 2002. Veto Threats as a Policy Tool: When to Threaten? *Presidential Studies Quarterly* 32: 30–45.

Dowd, Maureen. 1990. From President to Politician: Bush Attacks the Democrats. *New York Times*, October 30.

Edwards, George C., III. 1976. Presidential Influence in the House: Presidential Prestige as a Source of Presidential Power. *American Political Science Review* 70: 101–113.

————. 1989. *At the Margins: Presidential Leadership of Congress.* New Haven, CT: Yale University Press.

————. 1991. Presidential Influence in Congress: If We Ask the Wrong Questions We Get the Wrong Answers. *American Journal of Political Science* 35: 724–729.

Eizenstat, Stuart E. 1994. President Carter, the Democratic Party, and the Making of Domestic Policy. In *The Presidency and Domestic Policies of Jimmy Carter*, ed. Herbert D. Rosenbaum and Alexej Ugrinsky, 3–16. Westport, CT: Greenwood Press.

Fallows, James. 1979. The Passionless Presidency. *Atlantic Monthly* 243 (5): 33–47.

Farrell, John A. 2001. *Tip O'Neill and the Democratic Century*. Boston: Little, Brown, and Company.

Ferejohn, John. 1974. *Pork Barrel Politics: Rivers and Harbors Legislation, 1947–1968*. Stanford, CA: Stanford University Press.

Fink, Gary M., and Hugh Davis Graham, eds. 1998. *The Carter Presidency: Policy Choice in the Post-New Deal Era.* Lawrence: University of Kansas Press.

Flyvbjerg, Brent. 2006. Five Misunderstandings about Case-Study Research. *Qualitative Inquiry* 12 (2): 219–245.

Free, James. 1978. Is Carter Building Image at Expense of Congress? *The Birmingham News*, October 2.

Frisch, Scott A. 1998. *The Politics of Pork: A Study of Congressional Appropriation Earmarks*. New York: Garland.

Frisch, Scott A., and Sean Q Kelly. 2003. Don't Have the Data? Make Them Up! Congressional Archives as Untapped Data Sources. *PS: Political Science and Politics* 36 (2): 221–225.

————. 2006. Building Coalitions and Protecting Pork: The Case of the Tennessee–Tombigbee Waterway. Paper presented at the Northeastern Political Science Association meeting, November 2006, Boston.

Gilmour, John B. 2002. Institutional and Individual Influences on the President's Veto. *Journal of Politics* 64: 198–218.

Goldstein, Kenneth M. 1999. *Interest Groups, Lobbying, and Participation in America*. New York: Cambridge University Press.

Greene, Jennifer C., Valerie J. Caracelli, and Wendy F. Graham. 1989. Toward a Conceptual Framework for Mixed-Method Evaluation Design. *Educational Evaluation and Policy Analysis* 11: 255–274.

Groseclose, Tim, and Nolan McCarty. 2001. The Politics of Blame: Bargaining Before an Audience. *American Journal of Political Science* 45: 100–119.

Harris, Douglas B. 2007. Framing Legislative Debates: A View from the Party Leadership in the U.S. House of Representatives. Paper prepared for the Research Conference on Issue Framing, American University, June 2007, Washington, DC.

Heclo, Hugh. 1983. One Executive Branch or Many? In *Both Ends of the Avenue: The Presidency, the Executive Branch, and Congress in the 1980s*, ed. Anthony King, 26–58. Washington, DC: American Enterprise Institute.

Hird, John A. 1991. The Political Economy of Pork: Project Selection at the U.S. Army Corps of Engineers. *American Political Science Review* 85: 429–457.

Hoff, Samuel B. 1991. Saying NO: Presidential Support and Veto Use, 1889–1989. *American Political Quarterly* 19: 310–323.

Johnson, R. Burke, and Anthony J. Onwuegbuzie. 2004. Mixed Methods Research: A Research Paradigm Whose Time Has Come. *Educational Researcher* 33: 14–26.

Johnson, R. Burke, Anthony J. Onwuegbuzie, and Lisa J. Turner. 2006. Toward a Definition of Mixed Methods Research. *Journal of Mixed Methods Research* 1: 112–133.

Jones, Charles O. 1988. *The Trusteeship Presidency: Jimmy Carter and the United States Congress.* Baton Rouge: Louisiana State University Press.

———. 1998. *Passages to the Presidency: From Campaigning to Governing.* Washington, DC: Brookings Institution Press.

Jordan, Hamilton, 1994. Discussant: Hamilton Jordan. In *The Presidency and Domestic Policies of Jimmy Carter*, ed. Herbert D. Rosenbaum and Alexej Ugrinsky, 163–167. Westport, CT: Greenwood Press.

———. 2000. *No Such Thing as a Bad Day: A Memoir.* Marietta, GA: Longstreet Press.

Kauffman, Burton I., and Scott Kauffman. 2006. *The Presidency of James Earl Carter.* 2nd ed. Lawrence: University of Kansas Press.

Kernell, Samuel. 1997. *Going Public: New Strategies of Presidential Leadership.* 3rd ed. Washington, DC: Congressional Quarterly Press.

King, Gary, and Lyn Ragsdale. 1988. *The Elusive Executive: Discovering Statistical Patterns in the Presidency.* Washington, DC: Congressional Quarterly Press.

Krehbiel, Keith. 1998. *Pivotal Politics: A Theory of U.S. Lawmaking.* Chicago: University of Chicago Press.

Kumar, Martha Joynt. 2007. *The Contemporary Presidency*: The Carter White House Communications Operation: Lessons for His Successors. *Presidential Studies Quarterly* 37: 717–736.

Lee, Jong R. 1975. Presidential Vetoes from Washington to Nixon. *Journal of Politics* 37: 522–537.

LeLoup, Lance T. 2005. *Parties, Rules, and the Evolution of Congressional Budgeting.* Columbus: Ohio State University Press.

Maass, Arthur A. 1950. Congress and Water Resources. *American Political Science Review* 44: 576–593.

———. 1951. *Muddy Waters: The Army Engineers and the Nation's Rivers.* Cambridge, MA: Harvard University Press.

Mann, Robert. 1992. *Legacy to Power: Russell Long of Louisiana.* New York: Paragon.

Matthews, Steven A. 1989. Veto Threats: Rhetoric in a Bargaining Game. *Quarterly Journal of Economics* 104: 347–369.

McCool, Daniel. 1998. The Subsystem Family of Concepts: A Review and a Critique. *Political Research Quarterly* 51 (2): 551–570.

McCubbins, Mathew D. 1991. Government on Lay-Away: Federal Spending and Deficits Under Divided Party Control. In *The Politics of Divided Government*, ed. Gary W. Cox and Samuel Kernell, 113–154. Boulder, CO: Westview Press.

Merrill, F. T., Jr. 1977. How Carter Stopped Playing Politics and Started Having Trouble with Congress. *Washington Monthly*, July–August.

Mezey, Michael L. 1985. President and Congress: A Review Article. *Legislative Studies Quarterly* 10: 519–536.

Miller, Tim R. 1984. Politics of the Carter Administration's Hit List Water Initiative: Assessing the Significance of Subsystems in Water Politics. PhD diss., University of Utah.

————. 1985. Recent Trends in Federal Water Resource Management: Are the "Iron Triangles" in Retreat? *Policy Studies Review* 5 (2): 395–412.

Neustadt, Richard E. 1954. Presidency and Legislation: The Growth of Central Clearance. *American Political Science Review* 48: 641–671.

————. 1990. *Presidential Power and the Modern Presidents.* New York: The Free Press.

O'Neill, Tip, and William Novak. 1987. *Man of the House.* New York: Random House.

Ornstein, Norman, ed. 1981. *President and Congress: Assessing Reagan's First Year.* Washington, DC: American Enterprise Institute.

Pear, Robert. 2000. Clinton Details $2.4 billion in Widespread Reductions. *New York Times*, January 10, p. 12.

Polsby, Nelson W. 2004. *How Congress Evolves: Social Bases of Institutional Change.* Oxford, U.K.: Oxford University Press.

Powell, Jody. 1984. *The Other Side of the Story.* New York: William Morrow and Company, Inc.

Ransdell, Joseph E. 1916. The High Cost of the Pork Barrel. *Annals of the American Academy of Political and Social Science* 64: 43–55.

Reisner, Marc. 1993. *Cadillac Desert: The American West and Its Disappearing Water.* New York: Penguin Press.

Rohde, David W., and Dennis M. Simon. 1985. Presidential Vetoes and Congressional Response: A Study of Institutional Conflict. *American Journal of Political Science* 29 (3): 397–427.

Safire, William. 1993. *Safire's New Political Dictionary*. New York: Random House.

Savage, James D. 1988. *Balanced Budgets and American Politics*. Ithaca, NY: Cornell University Press.

Schick, Allen. 1995. *The Federal Budget: Politics, Policy, Process*. Washington, DC: Brookings Institution.

Skowronek, Stephen. 1997. *The Politics Presidents Make: Leadership from John Adams to Bill Clinton*. Boston: Belknap Press.

Stine, Jeffrey K. 1993. *Mixing the Waters: Environment, Politics, and the Building of the Tennessee–Tombigbee Waterway*. Akron, OH: University of Akron Press.

———. 1998. Environmental Policy during the Carter Administration. In *The Carter Presidency: Policy Choice in the Post–New Deal Era*, ed. Gary M. Fink and Hugh Davis Graham, 179–201. Lawrence: University of Kansas Press.

Sullivan, Terry. 1990. Bargaining with the President: A Simple Game and New Evidence. *American Political Science Review* 84: 1167–1195.

———. 1991a. Explaining Why Presidents Count: Signaling and Information. *Journal of Politics* 52: 939–962.

———. 1991b. The Bank Account Presidency: A New Measure and Evidence on the Temporal Path of Presidential Influence. *American Journal of Political Science* 35: 686–723.

———. 2001. Headcounts, Expectations, and Presidential Coalitions in Congress. *Journal of Politics* 63: 567–589.

Tolchin, Martin. 1977. Byrd Tells Carter Senate Is Angered by Unilateral Acts. *New York Times*, March 12, p. 1.

Wayne, Stephen J. 1982. Congressional Liaison in the Reagan White House: A Preliminary Assessment of the First Year. In *President and Congress: Assessing Reagan's First Year*, ed. Norman Ornstein, 44–65. Washington, DC: American Enterprise Institute.

INDEX

ABOUT THE AUTHORS

Scott A. Frisch is professor and chair of the political science program at California State University Channel Islands (CSUCI). Dr. Frisch received his BA from Lafayette College, a master's in government administration from the University of Pennsylvania, and a PhD in political science from the Claremont Graduate School. He served as a presidential management intern in the Department of Treasury and as a legislative assistant in the Office of Senator Frank Lautenberg of New Jersey. He joined the faculty at CSUCI after several years of teaching at California State University, Bakersfield, as well as East Carolina University. Dr. Frisch's primary research interests include Congress and the budgetary process. He is the author of the book *The Politics of Pork* (Garland Press, 1998).

• • •

Sean Q Kelly is associate professor of political science at California State University Channel Islands (CSUCI). Dr. Kelly received his BA from Seattle University, and his PhD in political science from the University of Colorado. He is a former American Political Science Association Congressional Fellow, during which he worked for the Senate Democratic Leadership. He joined the political science faculty at CSUCI in 2007 after teaching at Niagara University and East Carolina University. Dr. Kelly's primary research interests include American political institutions, political parties and leadership, and public policy. Dr. Kelly has authored and coauthored articles in several scholarly journals and edited volumes.

• • •

Dr. Frisch and Dr. Kelly are also the coauthors of *Committee Assignment Politics in the U.S. House of Representatives* (University of Oklahoma Press, 2006).

DATE DUE

BRODART, CO.　　　　　　　　　　　　　　　Cat. No. 23-221

CPSIA information can be obtained at www.ICGtesting.com
Printed in the USA
BVOW041311080112

280054BV00003B/3/P